Praise for *Ironbound*

"Darja does what she can to survive, and along the way, the sheer will and energy required for that survival costs her two marriages (one of them abusive), and a troubled son whose whereabouts are in question. Yet the resiliency of Majok's heroine is as persistent as her hold on her self-respect ... *Ironbound* is a reminder of the struggles of the immigrant experience, and of the dignity that those who brave it can achieve."

—David L. Coddon, *San Diego Union Tribune*

"*Ironbound* illuminates the American experience through the immigrant's journey. At a moment when the issue of immigration is being used as a political football, it's easy for some to distance themselves emotionally from the debate. But by holding us to the fire of Darja's story, *Ironbound* forces us to recognize the bitter reality of a system that renders invisible those hardworking casualties of the American dream."

—Charles McNulty, *Los Angeles Times*

"Unsentimental, Majok's *Ironbound* is a topical and insighful drama."

—Adam Feldman, *Time Out*

"A deceptively simple, thought-provoking, and elegant work of art ... Majok proves exceptional at writing a richly drawn character, Darja, who sheds light on the immigrant experience and the experience of the working poor ... The way Majok presents Darja's plight allows for some soul-searching on the larger socioeconomic issues at play in her work."

—Jennifer Perry, *Broadway World*

"An intriguing, humorous, contemporary play with a magnificent central role for a woman ... Darja is fully developed and self-reliant ... she's also smart ... she's also funny ... In Darja's case, in spite of the large themes suggested by the title, the political critique remains in the background; the play's heart is in the individual. She's a victim but also a tentative hero."

—Christopher Rawson, *Pittsburgh Post-Gazette*

Praise for *Sanctuary City*

"In plays like *Ironbound*, *Queens*, and now *Sanctuary City*, Majok writes about the plight of undocumented immigrants, with a glowering side-eye cast on the rest of us. Her unsparing, unsentimental vision of America is like Albee's of the country club set in *A Delicate Balance*: friendly to guests in theory, fiercely rejecting in fact."

—JESSE GREEN, *NEW YORK TIMES*

"The unrequited American promise inserts itself into any romantic story Majok writes . . . I think a clue to the way *Sanctuary City* operates is in the title. Its irony is meant to catch you up short."

—HELEN SHAW, *VULTURE*

"A tense, gripping play . . . No one who cares about contemporary American drama—or the millions of residents yearning for the ever more elusive American dream from the holding cell of their politicized limbo—should miss this play."

—CHARLES McNULTY, *LOS ANGELES TIMES*

"Hypnotic and heartbreaking . . . At a time of profound polarization on this delicate issue, Majok has given us something that transcends politics as only the best and most humane art can."

—ELYSA GARDNER, *NEW YORK STAGE REVIEW*

"One of the more distinctive voices to emerge among American dramatists in recent years . . . Majok's play is an urgently affecting chronicle of outsider immigrant experience that's political, intimately personal, and strangely apposite for our current moment."

—DAVID ROONEY, *HOLLYWOOD REPORTER*

"*Sanctuary City* triumphs on multiple levels: as an indictment of inhumane immigration policy and a social safety net in tatters, as a bildungsroman earnestly asking what the bonds and promises of childhood still mean just a few years later, as a one-of-a-kind doomed love story, where love can be selfish and unselfish all at once."

—LILY JANIAK, *SAN FRANCISCO CHRONICLE*

Ironbound &
Sanctuary City

OTHER BOOKS BY MARTYNA MAJOK PUBLISHED BY TCG

Cost of Living

Ironbound & Sanctuary City

TWO PLAYS

Martyna Majok

THEATRE COMMUNICATIONS GROUP
NEW YORK
2024

The publication of *Ironbound & Sanctuary City* by Martyna Majok, through TCG Books, is made possible with support by Mellon Foundation.

TCG books are exclusively distributed to the book trade by Consortium Book Sales and Distribution.

Library of Congress Control Numbers:
2023029429 (print) / 2023029430 (ebook)
ISBN 978-1-55936-976-3 (paperback) / ISBN 978-1-55936-945-9 (ebook)
A catalog record for this book is available from the Library of Congress.

Book design and composition by Lisa Govan
Cover design by Mark Melnick
Cover photograph by 4maksym/iStock by Getty Images
Author photograph by Josiah Bania

First Edition, January 2024

Contents

Ironbound

For Mama

There is an old story about a worker suspected of stealing: every evening, as he leaves the factory, the wheelbarrow he rolls in front of him is carefully inspected. The guards can find nothing. It is always empty. Finally, the penny drops: what the worker is stealing are the wheelbarrows themselves . . .

—SLAVOJ ŽIŽEK, *VIOLENCE*

Now near the end of the middle stretch of road
What have I learned? Some earthly wiles. An art.
That often I cannot tell good fortune from bad,
That once had seemed so easy to tell apart.

—ROBERT PINSKY, "JERSEY RAIN"

Darja (Marin Ireland) in the Rattlestick Playwrights Theater and Women's Project Theater coproduction. Photo: Sandra Coudert.

Ironbound had its world premiere at Round House Theatre (Ryan Rilette, Producing Artistic Director) in Bethesda, Maryland, as part of Women's Voices Theater Festival, on September 9, 2015. It was directed by Daniella Topol. The scenic design was by James Kronzer, the costume design was by Kathleen C. Geldard, the lighting design was by Brian MacDevitt and Andrew R. Cissna, the sound design and original music were by Eric Shimelonis; the dramaturg was Jessica Pearson and the production stage manager was Bekah Wachenfeld. The cast was:

DARJA	Alexandra Henrikson
TOMMY	Jefferson A. Russell
MAKS	Josiah Bania
VIC	William Vaughan

Ironbound had its New York premiere at Rattlestick Playwrights Theater (David Van Asselt, Artistic Director; Brian Long, Managing Director), in a coproduction with Women's Project Theater (Lisa McNulty, Producing Artistic Director; Maureen Moynihan, Managing Director), on March 16, 2016. It was directed by Daniella Topol. The scenic and lighting design were by Justin Townsend, the costume design was by Kaye Voyce, the sound design was by Jane Shaw; the production stage manager was Jaimie Van Dyke. The cast was:

DARJA	Marin Ireland
TOMMY	Morgan Spector
MAKS	Josiah Bania
VIC	Shiloh Fernandez

Ironbound was developed by Steppenwolf Theatre Company (Martha Lavey, Artistic Director; David Hawkanson, Executive Director) in Chicago, through its New Plays Initiative, and presented as part of its First Look Repertory of New Work in July 2014.

People

DARJA (dar-ya), twenty, thirty-four, forty-two
TOMMY, early forties
MAKS, thirties
VIC, a teenager

Place

A bus stop at night, a quarter mile from a factory in Elizabeth, New Jersey.
Or where there used to be a factory, depending on the year.
The play spans twenty-two years. In 2006, Darja is thirty-four.

Dialogistics

Slashes // indicate overlap.
Ellipses . . . are active silences.
(Non-italicized parentheses) within dialogue are meant to be spoken.

A Note on Staging

The play should be performed without an intermission.
Darja does not leave the stage until the very end of the play.

A Note on Performance

It can be tempting to play the circumstances of these characters' lives and end up missing the comedy. Self-pity has no currency here. Humor, however, has much. There is urgency and muscularity to these characters' needs to communicate. It is my hope for an audience to be disarmed—to laugh and understand.

A Note on New Jersey

The Jersey I know is gravel and cattails.
Empty quarter drinks and Buds litter parking lots. A marsh, a highway, bridges. Almost everyone is from somewhere else. And, yes, there's a reason they're not living in New York.

A Note on Polish Language

A translation and pronunciation guide for the Polish spoken in the play can be found at the end of this volume.

Scene One: 2014. Winter.

A streetlight zaps on.
Night. An environment of black.
Stars exist beyond smog; we don't see them.
A bus stop. Perhaps a faded sign. But probably not.
This world is one of constant less.
The chill of winter is just starting to set in.
Two people fight. Darja in sweats, a scarf, and a hoodie—the clothes
of a cleaning lady. She carries a large tote bag with her. Polish accent.
Tommy wears a Jersey Devils jacket over his postal worker's uniform.
Shorts. A tribal calf tat.

DARJA

What you don't understand is how so much you // hurt me.

TOMMY

I'm sorry!

DARJA

And I suppose to do with this what? What I suppose to do with this?

TOMMY

What you need to realize is it was from a different time. A Different Time.

DARJA

It was four month ago.

TOMMY

And I'm different now. Get in the car.

DARJA

Four month you keep from me and how many times we, since you, how many?

TOMMY

Can you please fuckin please get in the fuckin car please?

DARJA

This was not the week. This was not good week to do this.

TOMMY

I didn't do it this week. This week's the week you chose to find out about it.
Just get in the car. Yer not ridin that bus.

DARJA

I rode the other bus here.

TOMMY

And I tailed you in my—and that bus was not *this* bus, was not *this* neighborhood, waitin in *this*.

DARJA

I was riding that bus whole the time. Since that factory open, I ride.

TOMMY

Oh wow *that's* the factory you used to work at——?

DARJA

We are not having nice conversation now. The past. Memories. No.

TOMMY

(Trying) What happened to it // again?

DARJA

No.

. . .

TOMMY

Okay. Y'know what, Darja? What you gotta understand, man, is that people fuck up. It's planned that way. Yer Catholic. You know. It's planned this way for people to fuck up cuz if we were all perfect, fuck, who'd need to be Catholic. It's a cycle a system listen: we're not in control of these things, okay? Okay? We are Outta Control. And if you wanna crossify me for one little, man, after *everything* we've, everything *I've* done, for you, how many years?, if you wanna do that, Darja, then . . .

I don't know, man. I just don't think you should do that, Darja.

(Longer than it should take) I'm sorry.

DARJA

Me too.
Also you have no idea what you talking about, also.

TOMMY

The bus won't come. It's too late.

DARJA

And with rich lady, hey. Congratulation to you.

TOMMY

Did you hear me?

DARJA

It will come.

TOMMY

Fine, it comes, then what? You get off at Market and, what, walk?
Yer gonna walk through Newark now? A woman like you?

DARJA

I do this many year before you, Tommy.
A woman like what.

TOMMY

Get in the car.

DARJA

No.

TOMMY

DARJA GET IN THE FUCKIN CAR.

. . .

DARJA

You are not the one what gets to curse.

TOMMY

We're goin to the same place.

DARJA

And I pack when I get there.

TOMMY

Yer not gonna—

DARJA

No. You pack.

TOMMY

I'm not goin—

DARJA

No. Me. I am going.

TOMMY

Yeah? With what car?

DARJA

HEY! I had car.

TOMMY

Well you don't now, do you.

. . .

DARJA

I will find someone. I will find someone else.

TOMMY

Where?

DARJA

I found *you*. I was not blind person. I was not stupid. I know
exactly what was I doing so I was not stupid. I weighed you on
scale and I say mm Okay.

15

TOMMY

"Okay"?

DARJA

I am forty-two-years-old, married-twice-already woman: I have no time for stupid. So I weigh you on scale. Okay? So tell me, Tommy. How many times you—

TOMMY

What good's that kinda information?

DARJA

How many?

TOMMY

Why?

DARJA

Five? Four? One time every month?

TOMMY

Why do you need to know?

DARJA

Is some numbers I can handle. And some I probably cannot.

. . .

TOMMY

If you leave, I don't know what's gonna happen to me.

DARJA

Five?

TOMMY

I'm not good alone, you know that.

DARJA

Five?

. . .

TOMMY

Five.

DARJA

Not nine?

. . .

TOMMY

Nine.

DARJA

Not twelve?

TOMMY

No.

DARJA

Not twelve?

TOMMY

No.

DARJA

Not fourteen?

. . .

TOMMY

No.

DARJA

You look in my face and you lie. Why you lie my face when I find out things so good?

17

TOMMY

You never made a mistake?

DARJA

Fourteen times it's not mistake—

TOMMY

A very big // mistake—

DARJA

—fourteen times it's career.
Just answer me one thing. You want me I stay?

TOMMY

Yes. Yes, of course I, yes.

DARJA

Why.

TOMMY

I love you.

DARJA

NO. WE ARE NOT HAVING NICE CONVERSATION.

TOMMY

Well, you wanna know why, that's why.

DARJA

You love me, okay, but you consider leaving. You, so obvious, you
consider this—

TOMMY

I didn't *plan* // like— Things Happen.

DARJA

I TALK NOW.

Must be something what scares you more than leaving and so you stay. People imagine things. Things what can happen them, alone. In nights, they make pictures this thing in their heads. What you imagine? For me, is when I am cleaning her house and—

TOMMY

Does she know you know? About—that you know?

DARJA

What good would be if she know? I need job. And she have—*you* know—very dirty house.
No. She don't know.
You have broke me to one hundred pieces.

TOMMY

I'm sorry. How much you want me to apologize? I apologized. So much. It's in the past.

DARJA

What you imagine?

. . .

TOMMY

It's the nights. At the apartment. When yer workin late and no one's home.
Yer always workin. And late.
There's no sound.
And thoughts come.
I'm not good alone. You know that.

DARJA

And what happens if you can't fill apartment with someone?

TOMMY

I could find someone. But it's not about findin *some*one.

19

DARJA

Yes this is.

TOMMY

No. No, it's not. It's about *you* not leavin.

DARJA

Where? Where you would find someone? In *post office*? Go to someone's house? Slip to them *letter*? Slide in their mail slot your letter? "Meet me tonight."

TOMMY

I never slipped her a letter.

DARJA

Did I say you did?

TOMMY

That's not even my route. Montclair. Not my postal route.

If you think about it . . . I'm the best you ever had.

. . .

DARJA

This stupid bus. I am walking.

TOMMY

I'll just tail you, you start walkin.
HEY!—

(She has set out. He grabs her arm, stops her.)

Don't be fuckin crazy.
Okay?
Get in the car.

20

DARJA

Or you will just hold me like this until what?

(A moment.
He lets go.
A breath.)

What if I did to you what you did to me? What if?

TOMMY

I'd stay with you. And forgive you. And love you so very very much.

DARJA

You would stay with me, yes sure. Yes sure, because I make easy your life. For you, I cook, I clean, I lay there for you. I make sounds. Easy life. And you can whatever you want because I will lay there. Of course you would stay with me.

TOMMY

That's what you think?

DARJA

I weigh you on scale.

TOMMY

Well that's not what I think.
And, actually, you lay there very loudly.
Yer welcome.

DARJA

No, you are welcome.

Everything can change. You come home one day and maybe it's no one there. Everything it's already changed.

So what you will give me now?

TOMMY

What?

DARJA

What you will *give* me. For me to stay. Because you love me. So very very much. You think you can whatever you want with whoever you want for one night. One hour. Ten minutes (*I* know you). But everyone goes their homes after.

TOMMY

What is this "everyone" shit? It was One Person.

DARJA

And I know she have her home, her **kid, her husband**—rich husband—to go after. But you? What you have?

(Tommy inhales to reply.
No response.)

Okay. So what you will give?

. . .

TOMMY

I could . . . try to be more understanding—

DARJA

No. These it's fake ideas. Concrete, I need. Concrete. I need How Much You Will Give.

TOMMY

How much what?

DARJA

I need figures. Numbers. Money. You are not my great love, okay? You are not my great love for talking to me fake ideas.

TOMMY

Yer mine. Yer my great—

DARJA

We are not having nice conversation! I can't trust "understand-ing." I can't trust "try." I can trust three thousand dollars in my hands.

TOMMY

Three thousand!?!

DARJA

Dollars. In my bank. It's number I can trust.

TOMMY

Three thousand?

DARJA

At least.

. . .

TOMMY

So I give you three grand and you do what with it?

DARJA

Pay bills.

TOMMY

Not a car? Not buy a car?

DARJA

Maybe. Maybe I buy car.

TOMMY

You have no idea where he is.

. . .

DARJA

Does not matter what I buy.

TOMMY

It does if yer gonna take my money and run.

DARJA

You have three thousand dollars?

TOMMY

That's not the point.

DARJA

I think point is if you want me I stay or no. You have no kids, no house, one credit card. Car payments and rent you have.

TOMMY

The *majority* of rent.

DARJA

That it's all you have. I buy, I make, all your food. Laundry. Birth control! Birth control it's costing! How nice this is, only worry for yourself, no kids, just pay for yourself—

TOMMY

Aleks is twenty-five years—

DARJA

Two! Two! Aleks is twenty-two! It's two two's, how hard this is?

TOMMY

Twenty-anything, in my mind, makes you a grown-ass man. If he wants to go, he's gonna go. And he's gone.

DARJA

He it's not okay to go! You have three thousand dollars. You have more than three thousand dollars. What is for you three thousand dollars? Nothing. Is nothing for you.

. . .

I will come back. Okay?

TOMMY

You have no idea where he is.

DARJA

That's why I need three thousand shit dollars! I need one thousand for car so I can go find him and two thousand maybe for whatever he needs.

TOMMY

Rehab?

DARJA

Whatever he needs.

TOMMY

I told you I'm not payin for some deadbeat's kid.

DARJA

No, you paying me. You paying me to make noise.

TOMMY

You know how much rehab costs? Cuz that's what that kid needs.

DARJA

I can find something for cheap. Listen, you have broke me to millions pieces. You take my last good years I have in my life—

TOMMY

You were thirty-five when we got together.

DARJA

And you know how shit were the first thirty-five.

You don't wanna pay for my son, Tommy?, okay, it's fine. So just you pay for me and what money I make, I pay for my son. That's Fine. I say Fine to this before, I say Fine now. And right now I need car.

TOMMY

I'm not payin you to find him. So he can, fuckin, steal from me, trash our place. No, please, I'd love to see the cops again. Reconnect. I'd fuckin love it.

DARJA

For work, I need money for car.

TOMMY

No. If I give you money, I'd be payin you to stay. I mean I'd help *support* you. I'm not *payin* you like a, I'm not *payin* you. This would be me offerin you support. Cuz you know what, D? I respect you. You work hard. I respect you. It's not your fault where you were born. It's not your fault you were dealt a shit hand. All those Communists 'n' Nazis 'n' shit. But you came here. Home of the brave. Make a better—home of the brave! Even if you knew you'd be behind, you came. And that?: respect. That, from me, gets you respect. So if you need money, I can give you money. I can help you out. Not much, not three thousand dollars. But you'd need to stay.

. . .

DARJA

How much?

TOMMY

See, this is terrible right here. This is a terrible thing to talk about.

DARJA

How much or I am moving tomorrow.

TOMMY

You always threaten to move.

DARJA

And you listen then.

TOMMY

You never do.

DARJA

This time it's different.

TOMMY

Fine. Okay, fine, but for one mistake? For one mistake you'd trash it all?

DARJA

I counted seventeen times in four months with her. One time in 2013. Three in 2012, but this was someone else. "Allison." And in 2011, this was also someone else. "Courtney." And this is only counting times I know you go to meet with them.

Your phone has tap.
Since I know something is going on, it's have tap.
I listen every Monday to what I collect. While I clean Linda's house.

. . .

TOMMY

I put a password on my phone.

DARJA

Your mother's birthday. Backwards. Her birthday backwards.

. . .

TOMMY

You can't tap a cell—

DARJA

There is app.

. . .

. . .

TOMMY

So you know . . . how much exactly?

DARJA

I start in 2010. I start collecting things I can hold in my hands then.

TOMMY

And you waited til now.

DARJA

I was tired of lying.

TOMMY

Why'd you wait til now?

DARJA

I am tired of you lying.

. . .

. . .

TOMMY

You were holdin onto it? To tellin me you knew? For, what, for a rainy fuckin day?

DARJA

You pay or no?

TOMMY

Aleks left. He——

DARJA

No, // this is not about—

TOMMY

—he's never left before. He'd fuck shit up. Plenty. Torment you.
Me. But he never left. So you were waitin, huh? Til, what, til you
needed a trump? Til you really needed a fuckin bailout?

DARJA

This is just the situation.

TOMMY

He makes you cry.

DARJA

What?

TOMMY

Worse than I ever seen in a woman.
Why you hold onto him, he makes you fuckin cry?

. . .

DARJA

Two thousand. Just for car.

TOMMY

I don't do that. I don't make you cry.

DARJA

Just one thousand even.

TOMMY

I don't steal your car and run off for, how many, three days?, without a call. So you gotta take two buses to work. In this fuckin—
wasteland. I don't do that.

Shoulda tapped *his* phone, huh?

. . .

DARJA

Okay.
I leave you tomorrow.

TOMMY

Yeah? When the bus comes? Where's yer bus?
. . .
Huh, Darja? Where's yer bus?

. . .

DARJA

Just one thousand.
Tommy.
Seventeen times. In four months.
You owe me so much more than just one thousand.

TOMMY

I have pictures of you.

I have pictures of you doin things. To me. I have the video.
Remember the video? I said I erased it. I have it.

I could show it to people.

You can start makin demands when you got a leg to stand on.
Get in the car.

DARJA

("Nice try") No one here knows me. Show them.

(A challenge) No one in this country knows me.

. . .

Just——just one thousand?

Scene Two: 1992. Summer.

The sound of cicadas.
Darja and Maks. They wear shirts with sleeves, rolled up. Uniforms. Tags.
Sweat stains. A hot night. Maks is from the same country as Darja.
They count out their change. This is their game. Taking turns, they put
forward one coin from their respective pockets. That's one coin per turn,
chosen at random. Before them rests a small mass of coins.
Darja takes out a coin from her pocket, places it, sees what she got.
Then Maks takes out a coin from his pocket, places it, sees what he got.
And so the game goes.
The winner—the person who reaches bus fare first—gets a sexual favor
tonight.

MAKS

Five.

DARJA

. . . Ten.

31

MAKS

Twenty.

DARJA

Fourteen-five!

MAKS

Mm. Forty.

DARJA

What?

MAKS

Forty-five.

DARJA

("Jerk") Yes yes. Forty-five. Twenty, thirty, forty, yes okay.

MAKS

Fifty.

DARJA

Sixty.

MAKS

Eighty . . . five.

DARJA

One . . . ten.

MAKS

One . . . fifteen.

DARJA

Uh-oh. Close.

One . . . twenty.

MAKS

One twenty . . . one.

. . .

DARJA

Twenty-six!

MAKS

(Disbelief) No kurdy . . .

DARJA

I win! One twenty-six!

MAKS

No no, bus is costing more in nights.

DARJA

No no, I win!

MAKS

Yes yes. You win.

DARJA

Pay up.

MAKS

Now, pay up?

DARJA

I don't see anyone.

MAKS

Really? Now? Here?

DARJA

Do you see anyone . . .

33

(He gets down on his knees. She's loving this.)

MAKS

Dobra, to dziś zrobię Ci coś // co—

DARJA

You have to practice—

MAKS

So tonight I—

(He rides his hands up her thighs.)

Roztopię Cię, kobieto—

DARJA

Practice—

MAKS

I don't know how to say in English—

DARJA

Say: tonight you make me happy.

MAKS

Tonight—

DARJA

Because I win.

MAKS

Because you win, tonight I make you // happy.

DARJA

Tonight you make me happy.

MAKS

(Fifth time this week) Again.

DARJA

(Damn right) Again.

MAKS

(Damn right indeed) Again.

DARJA

(Pure joy) Again!

MAKS

You are too good this game.

DARJA

You are too good for me not to be this good this game.

(They kiss.
A car passes by, honks at them, trying to be funny.
They both flip it the bird, without taking their mouths off each other.)

You think rich people have this kinds games?

MAKS

They have other kinds games, rich people.

(They kiss. Just a little too long.)

DARJA

Maksiu, wait.
Tonight it's special night.

MAKS

(Still holding her, kissing her neck) Yeeeeaaahh it is.

DARJA

No no . . . I mean *yes* but . . . I have something tonight to tell you.
Look in my bag.

35

MAKS

Right now?

DARJA

Right now.

MAKS

. . . Right now?

DARJA

Right now!

(He looks in her tote bag.
Looks at her.
Looks at bag.
Looks at her.)

MAKS

You buy this?

DARJA

You funny.

MAKS

You . . .

DARJA

. . . rent this. Just for tonight. For special night.

(Maks pulls out a delicate nightgown.)

MAKS

From who?

DARJA

From woman I work for.

36

MAKS

Woman you, the crazy? She it's one-hundred-years-old woman, why you want this. And she it's crazy.

DARJA

She it's sick.

MAKS

She it's sick with crazy.

DARJA

She it's not wearing this. This it's from when she's just married, when she was nineteen years old. *I* am just married and I am *twenty* so really I am late to have something like this. I find in some box with tape on whole this thing. These people always are throwing beautiful things. She can't to throw this beautiful thing. Look at this.

(He feels the nightgown. Flower petals.)

Is just for tonight. She will never know.

MAKS

What if she does?

DARJA

. . . She it's crazy.
Is just for this night.

MAKS

She it's crazy?

DARJA

You talking so much. You will not be talking so much tonight.

(She models it against herself.)

Maksiu.

37

                                    MAKS

Bring this back.

                                    DARJA

Why?

                                    MAKS

I want you wear something what's for you.

                                    DARJA

And this it's not for me?

                                    MAKS

It's, no, this it's not for you, you stole this.

                                    DARJA

So, okay, I give this back. After tonight.

                                    MAKS

No, Darju, ty nie rozumiesz—

                                    DARJA

English.

                                    MAKS

(Dismissal) Ah.

                                    DARJA

You will never go no place you don't speak English.

                                    MAKS

Yeah? I speak English whole time am here. Since I come here,
I speak English. You know who else speaks English? Whole rest
this country. Is nothing special you speak English this country.

You don't *take* things like some bullshit person. Bring this back.
. . .

I buy for you one.
One day.

(They stand in silence.
Then he takes out liquor. Swigs.)

You want?

MAKS

DARJA

No.

MAKS

Now you mad?

DARJA

I just don't want drink.

MAKS

Why?

DARJA

I just don't.

MAKS

You steal but you don't drink. What sense is this.

DARJA

Why that is not for me?

MAKS

You did not buy it.

DARJA

What if she give to me this?

MAKS

She did not give to you that.

39

                            DARJA

She throw this away, same thing like if she give me. I am wearing
her clothes sometimes. When I push her in wheelchair, I wear her
hats so if she turn around her head, I can fast take this off. When
I shop for her food, I wear her scarf. When I take her bills to post
office. Sometimes I even walk in Central Park—just for like, little
bit—in her dress. Beautiful dress. Blue. I take this off before I go
inside and clean her furnitures. But people on the street . . . in
life . . . they for some reason they always know who am I. I wear
her clothes but.

Maks.
Why you think we look poor?

                            MAKS

Because we don't look rich.
You wait. You have one day rich husband.

                            DARJA

You are divorcing me?

                            MAKS

You are not funny.

                            DARJA

Yes I am.

(He takes out a cigarette, lights.)

                            MAKS

Want?

                            DARJA

No.

                            MAKS

No?

DARJA

No.

MAKS

No?

DARJA

No.

. . .

MAKS

No?

DARJA

No!

MAKS

Who are you?

DARJA

Is too hot.

MAKS

To smoke is?

DARJA

Too hot to smoke, yes.

MAKS

You okay maybe?

DARJA

I am fine thank you very much and yourself?

MAKS

(*"Suit yourself"*) Okay.

(He smokes.
They stare out, waiting for the bus.)

Late, yes?

DARJA

(Terrified; taken aback) What?

. . .

MAKS

The bus.
Late.
Yes?

DARJA

Yes.
Late.

The bus.

(Maks smokes.)

I love this smell.

MAKS

You can have one.

DARJA

No. I can't.

MAKS

Why you can't?

DARJA

No.

. . .

MAKS

This waiting is bullshit. I want car.

DARJA

Yes.

MAKS

One day.

DARJA

I want house.

MAKS

Maybe.

DARJA

You don't want house?

MAKS

I want to know we can go anyplace we want.

DARJA

(Not smiling) Chicago?

MAKS

(Smiling) Chicago!

DARJA

Please don't do it.

(Too late. Maks has taken out his harmonica.
He plays.
He sings the chorus of "Czerwony Jak Cegła" by Dżem—a Polish blues song.
He's damn good. He shines.
Darja, however, is having none of it.
This feels like the five hundredth time he is doing this.)

MAKS

(Singing) Czerwony jak cegła—

DARJA

(This always happens) Okay.

MAKS

(Singing) —rozgrzany jak piec, Muszę mieć, // muszę ją mieć—

DARJA

Yeah okay.

MAKS

Czerwony jak cegła, rozgrzany jak piec,
Fuck this bus,
Oh yeeeeaaaaahhhh, fuck this bus.

(He plays, takes her, gets her to dance. She enjoys it in spite of herself.
He finds his way into her hair, her neck. Turns into a close, slow dance.
He sings or hums the song slower, into her. It's wonderful. Then she slips
out of the dance.)

DARJA

Yes, very nice. You sing very nice. Not like most nice in whole the
world but nice.

MAKS

Me and Clinton, we will play together one day.

DARJA

Amazing: The Wall falls down; American Dream falls in. Everyone
thinks they can be star now. Amazing.

MAKS

It's only American, dreams?

DARJA

Blues it's American.

MAKS

Okay and but this song they write in Poland so.

DARJA

No one understands you.

MAKS

They will understand. It's blues. It's Chicago.

DARJA

There it's Black people there play blues, Chicago.

MAKS

See?, so I can be like, New Thing.
Sing.

DARJA

I am not singer.

MAKS

No, you are not singer but you can sing. All people can sing. You can't sing means you are died.

DARJA

I work in factory. That it's what I do. And I clean old woman.

MAKS

And steal her clothes. You can't tell me you don't want more.

DARJA

I do. Yes, Maks. I do, very much, want more.

MAKS

Okay so this is why we go Chicago. I can spend whole my life in
this place lifting, pushing. But one song? Good song?

And you know all good music it's come from poor people.

DARJA

And if this don't work?

MAKS

What?

DARJA

Your one song?
Good song?

(This is the first time she's voiced this.)

MAKS

It just will.

DARJA

And what we will do now?

MAKS

Why it's all this questions?

DARJA

I just think we should think.

MAKS

Think what.

DARJA

Think if maybe . . . think what if maybe . . . in case . . .

MAKS

What.

DARJA

We need more money.

MAKS

Because you want, what— *(Indicates nightgown)* things like this?

DARJA

We can't live always like how we live now. We need money. Now.

MAKS

Okay but what more I can do? I speak English. I have job and I work this all the time. And I am beautiful.

DARJA

What this means, you—

MAKS

So in America, if you beautiful, they give to you jobs. Take two people, put them next each other, both speak English, and, see?, our boss he take the beautiful. You can never be ugly or we will starve. Or fat. Never also be fat.

DARJA

Ania it's not beautiful—not anymore—and she have job. Ania lose her arm and she have job. Is *because* she have job that she lose her arm. And *because* she lose her arm, she keep job. Funny mathematics.

MAKS

("Stop talking") Okay—

DARJA

You see her? They take skin from her here *(Indicates stomach)* this skin they take to make the arm again. I see her ... how she say this ... button. I see her button on her new arm when she shake hands.

MAKS

But she get money. They take care of this.

DARJA

She get money but not so much money. Not like, what this costs to have arm. And she get to keep her job in factory. With us. Hoorah.

MAKS

(Looking around) Okay, *może teraz nie jest // najlepszy czas*—

DARJA

Anyone here it's Polish so who you think you keeping secrets from speaking Polish?

MAKS

Okay. You know what? Maybe you forget how should you act with me.

DARJA

Maybe you too you forget. You want to be big man? Have me act to you like you big man? Okay. So I want more, Maks. I need insurance. Apartment. *Out* of basement apartment. Car. I want car.

MAKS

Okay.
One day.

DARJA

I want more than anything car.

MAKS

Then this is sad life.

DARJA

There will one day be when you have to put away this songs.

(Maks lights another cigarette.)

Don't smoke this by me.

MAKS

You said you "love."

DARJA

I don't want smoke by me.

MAKS

So don't make me mad, I don't smoke. This it's what you have tonight to tell me? How much I don't give you? Thank you. Thank you so very much.

(They stand silent.)

Is music in my head right now. You should know this. And this it's what I do when bus it's late or when someone skin it's rip from bones. Or when my wife she say to me am nothing. Don't try to take this from me.

(They stand apart a little while longer. Facing forward.
Then she moves to him. Rests against him, holds his hand, wraps it around her waist.
But something doesn't quite fit.
They stare forward.)

Is good to have thing like this. For some reason you think is bad but is good. I watch people. Singers. Not here because we don't go places but . . . home. I watch faces them when they sing. They look . . . pain sometimes. Eyes closed. Mouth big, red. And maybe you don't see this but what I see it's . . . it's something in them . . . when they sing . . . it's like escaping them. Something leaves their mouth what makes inside them red, what burns. Is something hot, something loud, something maybe bad.

Think what things he maybe do if he could not get this out. Something maybe bad.

I come from shit, okay?, and I—

DARJA

And me?

MAKS

And we come *to* this shit. But we have something. We are not just body. Lift. Pull. Push. We are more than this.

DARJA

Well no one pays us for this "more."

MAKS

You can burn money. Gone, two seconds. Money it's nothing. Is important. But is nothing. What's most important in this life it's this thing you have what no one can take from you.

DARJA

I can't think what's something can't someone take.

MAKS

Then you make one. One thing what's yours in whole this world. People try to take, you fight.

DARJA

I am fighting.

MAKS

Cars break.

. . .

I have music. People need to know this.

DARJA

I know this.

MAKS

People in this country need to know this so I don't fall from this world like nothing ever happen.

DARJA

I know this. And I know you. I know only you here. In whole country. In whole country, really, I have only you.

MAKS

And is many things can happen to me.

. . .

Don't try to take this from me.

(He smokes. She watches him.)

. . .

DARJA

We need money this week. Little extra.

MAKS

Because see?, again money. Whole this time we talk, it's money.

DARJA

This week, we need.
And maybe for few months.

MAKS

Why.

DARJA

To go to doctor.

. . .

MAKS

You feel sick?

DARJA

No.

. . .
. . .
. . .

(Maks knows.
He looks at her.
Looks forward.
A worried face.
They look forward.)

. . .

There is the bus.

Scene Three: 2014. Winter.

Headlights.
A car horn blares from a distance. Closer. Closer.
A car skids. Stops.
Car door opens, slams shut.
Tommy enters in his postal uniform, frazzled.

TOMMY

The fuck's the matter with you!?!

DARJA

You were not stopping.

TOMMY

What if I didn't see you? It's fuckin dark out!

DARJA

You have your lights.

TOMMY

The fuck is your problem?

DARJA

You are happy you did not hit me?

(Tommy catches his breath.)

TOMMY

I coulda // fuckin—

DARJA

I know what you could. Calm down. Everything it's okay.
How are you?

TOMMY

Are you fuckin kidding?

DARJA

Calm down.

TOMMY

Why were you standin in the middle of the road?!

DARJA

I know which way you come home.

TOMMY

And you couldn't just see me at home?

DARJA

You pass me in your car, standing this bus stop, two nights, and
you never stop to give me ride.

TOMMY

You said you didn't want one, made that pretty clear.

DARJA

AND SO WHAT THE FUCK IS WRONG WITH YOU FOR
LISTENING.

. . .

How . . . how damnit are you, is why I stop you, how are you. Two
days already we don't talk, no hello when I come home, nothing.

So. How are you.

TOMMY

This how you apologize?

DARJA

Who apologize?, *me?*

TOMMY

(Moving to exit back to car) Right.

DARJA

TOMMY HOW ARE YOU.

TOMMY

(Turning back) I'M HUNGRY. I JUST FINISHED WORK.

DARJA

WHAT YOU WOULD LIKE FOR DINNER.

TOMMY

Are we playin now?
. . .
I got plans for dinner. I was goin home to change.

DARJA

Where you going?

                    TOMMY

Some Italian place.

                    DARJA

Which one?

                    TOMMY

No.

                    DARJA

With "Linda"?

                    TOMMY

My new password's good, right?
Yes. With Linda.

                    DARJA

Mm. Linda. It's fancy?

                    TOMMY

You jumped in front a my car for a restaurant recommendation?

                    DARJA

Sure why not?, since you expert.

                    TOMMY

Look if you got a problem with what I'm doin, you can leave. You
can pack and leave like you keep threatenin to—

                    DARJA

I don't want to leave.

                    TOMMY

You want *me* to leave then?

                    DARJA

No.

TOMMY

You know what I'm doin, you don't want me to leave?

DARJA

No.

TOMMY

You gonna ask me questions, where I'm goin, what Italian place?

DARJA

No . . . Am just—

TOMMY

What? You gonna come there and, fuckin, mace her, what?

DARJA

No.

TOMMY

Assault her?, I know you.

DARJA

No. Am just . . . curious.
I like to imagine. Just curious.
What you will eat?

TOMMY

I don't know yet.
(Really thinks about this a second, then) Pasta.

DARJA

Why you ask I would do this? Why you think I could be like this?
Mean like this? I am not like this. Violence. I don't "mace" people.

TOMMY

Fine. Yer right.

DARJA

I find other things to do to people.

. . .

TOMMY

What did you do?

DARJA

Did you know I lose all of them?

TOMMY

Wait, what did you do?

DARJA

All my houses, I lose. All my jobs. She call to every woman I work
for. Every one. She tell to them I "damage." I "damage" things.
Yeah okay but what she did not to tell them is why, why I "damage" things.

TOMMY

Did you do something to Linda?

DARJA

Not to her, to stupid her. Her things. Her clothes. The bras, the
underwears. Dresses. // Few dresses.

TOMMY

Darja.

DARJA

And I drink her wine. The most dusty one.

TOMMY

What did you do to her things?

DARJA

What you think, I burn them.

TOMMY

Like, up? You burned them up?

DARJA

Yes, up. Away. No more.

TOMMY

The woman's a damn millionaire // and you just burned her shit up?

DARJA

Her *husband* it's millionaire and // she it's sick nasty inside his house—

TOMMY

Jesus fuckin— Is it still burning?

DARJA

Was beautiful. And so was her clothes. You know I think first maybe I keep all this things but then I think No. I don't know what she does in this things. Dirty dirty nasty sick. She want I clean her house? I clean the bitch's house.

(Darja finds this hilarious. Until she doesn't.
Tommy watches a woman laugh about arson.)

TOMMY

This is hilarious to you?

DARJA

Tommy, I have no job!

TOMMY

Did you think you would?

DARJA

I have NO job!

TOMMY

Welcome to America. Get another one.

(At some point, Tommy takes out his phone to make a call.)

DARJA

How? Please tell to me how. You see peoples here they go to school years, *years* they go, and they don't have nothing now. What I can do? Even the ugly jobs they don't have no more. Look there. Look the factory there. Just empty and glass. No factories here, nothing. No car. What I can do?

TOMMY

Maybe you shoulda sold her fuckin shit instead of burnin it.

. . .

DARJA

You know what?
Yes.
Yes, fuck. Yes, I should.

TOMMY

Prob'ly insured.

DARJA

Damnit fuck.

(Darja, a little lost in the sobering reality of it all, looks at the rubble of the factory, but speaks to Tommy, who is dealing with his phone.)

These people, if they could, they would send they houses to China to be cleaned. But we work til day our body breaks. Til place close or I close, I work and I barely—

TOMMY

(On the phone, leaving a sexy message) Hey yeah it's the uh, The Pool Guy. Callin about yer uh, pool. Just callin to check in uh *confirm* that I'm still doin yer pool. Tonight. *(Extra sexy)* Call me back.

(He hangs up. Darja looks at him.)

DARJA

Tommy—

TOMMY

Listen, I don't exactly owe you anything. Except rent. I owe you half the rent while we're still livin together and I left it on the table this morning—

(She kisses him abruptly.
He doesn't move away.
But he doesn't respond much either.)

DARJA

What time you are meeting her?

TOMMY

I got time. A little time.

DARJA

You could drive any other different way back home. But you drive here. By my bus. Where I stand.

TOMMY

This is just the way home.

DARJA

You came out the car.
You try to make me jealous? Hm, Pool Guy?

TOMMY

Why, *are* you jealous? Firestarter?

. . .
. . .

DARJA

So how you are doing?

TOMMY

Good. Considering. Good.
. . .
. . . And yourself?

DARJA

Good.
Considering.
. . .
And work?

TOMMY

Oh work is—you know.

DARJA

They are, maybe they are, hiring? At . . . at post—?

TOMMY

No. I don't think so, no. Budget cuts. Budget cuts all over the place.
People don't mail. I'm lucky to still, y'know. Fuckin internet.

DARJA

Yes.

TOMMY

Fuckin email.

                    DARJA

Yes.

(She kisses him again. Maybe it's more of a mutual one this time.)

I can make pasta.
Let's go home.

(Tommy considers. He sees what she's doing and is conflicted.
He softly extricates himself from her embrace.
It's not easy for him to ask her this.)

                    TOMMY

You think yer gonna stay at the apartment?

                    DARJA

I —what?
I, yes, I think I should have enough. Maybe.
For next month.
But maybe you can just—

                    TOMMY

I mean, after. Like will you be there after next month.
After the lease's up.

                    DARJA

I have to.

                    TOMMY

You have to?

                    DARJA

Yes, I have to.

                    TOMMY

"In case he comes back"?

DARJA

He it's not picking up my calls. If Aleks comes back, I should be
there.

TOMMY

You go to the police?

DARJA

Yes.

TOMMY

Missing kid or stolen car?

DARJA

Missing kid.

TOMMY

Shoulda told em stolen car.

DARJA

I miss // him——

TOMMY

The *car's* never fucked you over.

. . .

DARJA

I miss him very much.

. . .

TOMMY

Listen I'm sorry for what I'm about to but, I kinda, gotta since it's
just a few weeks really til we gotta decide about the, listen.

Can you afford the rent?

DARJA

I said I think I—

TOMMY

On yer own?

DARJA

Why.

TOMMY

Cuz look I'm not gonna throw you out—

DARJA

Why you would throw me out.

TOMMY

I said I wouldn't, I would Not Throw You Out.
But—

DARJA

What.

TOMMY

Just. Can you afford rent?

DARJA

. . . Yes.
Somehow.
Maybe.
Tommy, I don't have car so where I can go anyway, how I can move.

TOMMY

There's vans. Trucks.

DARJA

Yeah okay, what money I have for, and I have things, big things
what are mine in the apartment.

TOMMY

Not that many. The furniture's mine.

DARJA

What you try to do?

TOMMY

I need to know whether to start lookin for a place or—

DARJA

Why you look for place?

TOMMY

Y'know what, I'll just start lookin for a place. I don't need that extra room. Save a few that way. I'll just look and you can tell me what you wanna do. Or tell Jim. You can talk to Jim about the lease.

DARJA

Why it's lease? Why money? Furniture, numbers. Why these things, all these *things*?

TOMMY

As opposed to what?

DARJA

To . . . more.

TOMMY

More what?

DARJA

Okay. Okay. You are playing now.

TOMMY

I don't know what yer talkin about, "more." You tap my phone. You destroy my girlfriend's shit—

DARJA

Girlfriend?

TOMMY

And you freeload.
So more what. What more is it you want?

DARJA

I don't know.

TOMMY

Well. If you don't know, I don't know.

DARJA

My second husband would say this.

TOMMY

He talked? I thought he'd just beat the shit out of you.
. . .
I'm sorry. I'm sorry I'm bein a fuckin jerk. I just, I can't have you
fuckin shit up for me.

DARJA

Like what?

TOMMY

If what we had was different, you and me—

DARJA

We're together six almost seven years.

TOMMY

Livin together, we been, for six almost seven years.

DARJA

And so that's just nothing?

TOMMY

I dunno. You tell me. Was that a real kiss?
Was that you kissin me fer real there or putting in an application
fer the post office?

DARJA

For real, Tommy.

TOMMY

Yeah well I dunno. There's just some shit now, with us, that I don't
know.

DARJA

And so what it's this with "Linda" now you have? This is real?

TOMMY

I don't know exactly.
Yet.
But I'd like to find out. She's not happy in her marriage and we
// been—

DARJA

("That's enough") Okay.
("You fucking idiot") Okay.
. . .
(Sees he's serious) Okay.

TOMMY

You don't hafta tell me now but, just lemme know what you
wanna do. About the apartment.
Okay?
Sorry.

(He looks at her.
She's looking away. At the factory.)

DARJA

There was once woman at that factory—

TOMMY

Darja.

DARJA

They close this factory. First people they go or they let go and now they just, everything from China so—

TOMMY

Yeah that happens. Listen, I gotta // get goin—

DARJA

I can be fast.
Six, almost seven years . . .
And then you . . . and then you can . . .

There was woman. My friend. She was my friend. She, one day, she gets her sleeve catch in machine. It's paper factory and she work on one machine we use to cut papers. And this machine it slice her arm like paper. Layers. Like paper. The bone is left.

They tell to us, first day, they say we be careful this machine. They tell to us we be *so* careful, we must be scared this machine. It can do many things to us. We must be scared always so we do not sleep and nothing happens us. It was so loud in this place, we wear plugs our ears. So when she was screaming . . .

We do not hear her.
No one hears.
I ask her how she could let this to happen to her. How she can forget to be scared.

She say me she could not remember what she was thinking . . . but she remembers for one moment she was thinking *something*.

She don't tell to me what this was. But I know.
She was thinking being not here.

She was thinking someplace, something, what was not for her. Or she would see when her sleeve it's catching and her arm it's taking. Because that's where she is, she is here. Like me.

I am not good person.

I am not good person also. I don't know who I think I am to say to you things. I don't know why I judge you. And you help me before. You help me before in bad times. After my second husband. After he . . .

I don't know how I will make it next month. How I will . . . And if I have to move . . . I . . . I don't know what to do. Truly. I . . . I don't know. I am sorry. I am sorry for that I do bad things to you.

(Longer than it should take) I love you very much.

. . .

TOMMY

I gotta go.

DARJA

Can we go to dinner?

TOMMY

I'm already goin to dinner.

DARJA

Tomorrow?

TOMMY

I'm gonna keep seein this woman.

DARJA

. . .

TOMMY

I'm not gonna stop.

DARJA

. . .

TOMMY

I like her.

. . .

That doesn't bother you?

. . .

. . .

DARJA

No.

Just maybe sometimes we can go to dinner?

(Tommy's cell phone rings.
Rings.
He resists picking it up in front of Darja.)

Pick it up.

. . .

. . .

Pick it up.

(It rings until it goes to voice mail. Or until he sends it to voice mail.)

Her car costs more than you make in three years. What you think will happen? She leave her husband for you and your Honda?

TOMMY

(Moving to exit) Have a // good night.

DARJA

(Follows after Tommy) She move in with you? What you can give this woman? What you think it's so special in *you*?

TOMMY

I'm not doin this right now.

(Darja gets in Tommy's face, blocks his exit.)

DARJA

You know what you—HEY!—you know what you are? You are
toy for her. Pool toy. She it's bored and there you are. "Girlfriend"? You are fucking dreaming. You never will be for her
more. You will never be more.

TOMMY

You done?

(Darja attacks Tommy.
He restrains her.
Pushes her away from him.
They stand apart.
This has never happened before between them.)

Don't ever fuckin wonder.

DARJA

What.

TOMMY

Why yer life's been what it's been.

(Tommy moves to exit. Remembers something.)

Three weeks.

DARJA

Don't worry. Am gone tonight.

TOMMY

Okay then.
Take fuckin care.

(Tommy exits.)

Scene Four: 2006. Fall.

Very late night. The stage should feel a little different.
Darja is badly bruised.
She looks as though she's traveled a far distance from someplace.
She may have just come from across the street, from the factory, but there is deep weathering to her. She looks for some cardboard, some debris, to make a bed. A dirty tire is her pillow.
She takes her coat off, lays it down, lays on it.
It's too cold.
She puts it back on.
She takes off her scarf, lays it on the tire to cushion her face.
She is about to lay down when she remembers something.
She takes out a small votive candle. And a lighter.
Lights the candle.
And places it nearby her.
She does the sign of the cross.
And lays down.
A car passes.
A car stops.

And a car drives off.
A young man, Vic, enters. Skull cap, hoodie, jeans, tattoos. He's physi-
cally frail under his many layers, but he acts like brick. He considers
something in his hands as he enters.
He sees a body on the ground and quickly stuffs the thing in his pocket.
He walks up to Darja, protective of this, his turf.
He stands over her.

VIC

'Ey.
'Ey, man.
'Ey, man, you cool?
You cool?
You dead?

DARJA

please no

VIC

(Seeing it's a woman) Oh shit.

DARJA

please

VIC

(Seeing her face) Oh shit, man.

DARJA

please I have no money

VIC

Yeah, man, I figured.

Listen, yer not tryin to sleep out here tonight, are you? Cuz I'ma
tell you right now that ain't the dopest of thoughts.

DARJA

What?

74

VIC

'Ey man, don't cry.

DARJA

Is just my face.

VIC

You look like you need some ice or somethin.

DARJA

No.

VIC

I could get you ice.

DARJA

Is enough cold for me.

VIC

QuickChek ain't far.

DARJA

No please thank you no. Thank you. I am thirty-four-years-old woman. I can take care myself.

VIC

Um, lady?, you nappin on a tire.

. . .

Holy shit, man. Yer like . . . holy . . . shit . . . yer like A Battered Woman. Yer like a legit battered woman.

DARJA

Am sorry. I go.

VIC

Nah, man, nah. Sorry, I'm just, y'know, I'm like, Takin Stock. This is some crazy shit right here I'm seein. This really happens. Shit.

(He stares at her a little too long.)

I mean, I mean if you know where to go, y'know, like a women's place or somethin, man, then go, go, you should totally go. But I mean you don't *gotta* go. *(Checks his pager/phone)* Not yet.

(Vic spots the lit candle on the ground.)

You workin on some *ambience* there?

DARJA

What?

VIC

Shit, should I not try 'n' make you laugh? It hurt yer face?

DARJA

The bus it's not coming.

VIC

What? Yeah, I know.

DARJA

Not this late.

VIC

Nope. Nope prob'ly not. Were you waitin for the bus?

DARJA

No I just say you in case *you* coming here for waiting.

VIC

Me? Man, I ain't waitin on no bus, man, nah.

DARJA

So what you come for?

VIC

Things.
Business.
Sales.
. . .
Things.

(He stares too long.)

DARJA

I have papers. Not with me now but I have.

VIC

I look like a cop?

DARJA

You are very questions. You very questions and little answers to
be just standing here in the night waiting where is no one around
to—oooooh. Oh okay. I know what you are.

VIC

Yeah? What am I?

DARJA

Yeah okay I know.

VIC

Okay. Well, the thing you think I am . . . it bother you?

DARJA

We all of us need money.

VIC

Not a bad way to make it, I'ma tell you that.

DARJA

Yeah okay I don't think so I agree but.

We are different peoples.

You say you know women's place?

VIC

I know *of* em. That they got em. I'd assume they would around *here*.

What's the name of the stairs fucked you up?

DARJA

Excuse?

VIC

Who fucked you up?

DARJA

Why?

VIC

Okay. You don't trust me. But so it was your husband?, boyfriend?

DARJA

Why.

VIC

Father?, yer son?

DARJA

No. Not my son. No.

VIC

Oh, shit! That is Fucked Up. It was your son?

DARJA

No! Not my son! Why you saying things my son! What the fuck it's your problem saying things you don't know. This it's how people gets to trouble. You kinds people you stay away my son.

. . .
. . .
. . .

VIC

Whoa.
Okay.
Arright, man. Okay.

But listen. I roll up to, fuckin, this place might as well be *Detroit*, at one A.M. and I see a fuckin lady turnin in on the ground. A *lady*. Fuckin, tuckin herself in on this hepatitis ground. Shiner like a, *damn*. And you want me just to roll right out like the world don't affect me?

DARJA

Why it's only for lady you stop?

VIC

Woman, are you serious?, someone could—hold up, what you mean like instead of for a man? What, you think I got like intentions?

DARJA

I don't know what you got.

VIC

Man, that's how men get into fuckin trouble. Don't be throwin no *intentions* on me. I'm talkin bout other kinds a men, the shit other kinds a men could do if they find you just laid out here like a free pile a cash.

You would know. Right?

Shit, try to get you ice, try to talk, be nice 'n' shit. Fuck. 'N' you do me like that? tsss okay.

DARJA

Was my husband. Was my husband did to me this. Happy?

VIC

Yo but why'd he hit you? Was he drunk?

DARJA

Why you asking whole these questions me?

VIC

It happen a lot?

DARJA

Why you asking?

VIC

Yo where you from like, Russia?

DARJA

(Offended) NO.

VIC

So you from like a Little Russia then like one of them Bosnias or—oh shit. OH. SHIT. Were you like . . . *trafficked*?

DARJA

What?

VIC

Like . . . *trafficked*?
. . . In like a sexual // kinda way?

DARJA

I used to work there. Okay? That factory. When I was working there, I remember sometimes they don't close back door when they do delivery. So I think I go there, sleep there—

VIC

You got no place to sleep?

DARJA

No yes I have but—

VIC

Gotcha. Right.

DARJA

But now some asshole he put lock so. Here I am.

Don't call to no one, okay? My husband, he was my boss there. My second husband, he was boss. Before this place close. He used to manage whole that building.

VIC

And now he . . . ?

DARJA

Does not.
How you come here? You have car maybe?

VIC

Nah, man, shit, I wish I had a car, nah. Where you need to go?

DARJA

Home.

VIC

Yeah, I'ma say that's prob'ly not the best thought either.

DARJA

This was not best thought also.

VIC

You wanna get a hotel?

DARJA

Excuse?

VIC

Just, to sleep in.

DARJA

I . . .
. . . I have no money.

VIC

You need money? *(Off her look)* Whoa, man. It ain't even like that.

DARJA

How it's like so?

VIC

I mean, I *got* money.

DARJA

Yeah you got but . . . *how* you got . . . can't be so good.

VIC

You about to sleep in the street and you really gonna get moral on me right now, ma?

DARJA

Why you call // me this?

VIC

It's just how we do // out here, nah'mean.

DARJA

How who?, // who "we"?

VIC

Well what's yer name then. What's yer name.

(She considers.
Then——)

DARJA

Darja.

VIC

Yeah? I'm Vic.

(Vic offers her a fist bump.
A pause.
She has no idea what to do with this.
Eventually, somehow, Darja "bumps" back.
Though it's probably more a slap on the fist. Something unexpected.
This ignites a rap explosion.)

(Rap) Vic Vic the Slick. Yeah, Vic the Brick. Yeah, Vic the Vic the Buttery Buttery Bisquick. I got a good name for this, right? I'm the Marinara on yer Mozzarella Stick. Corner Kick on a Hat Trick. Don't need a Sidekick OH SHIT is that a Deer Tick? Salt Lick. Toothpick. Saint Nick.

(Darja's stone serious.)

See it's just I don't wanna make you laugh, y'know, cuz a yer face. So I'm not even tryin to make you laugh.

DARJA

. . . Card Trick.

VIC

Politick! You lightnin quick!

. . .

DARJA

. . . Stick.

(Darja smiles. Then grabs her face.)

("Ow") Joj.

VIC

Oh shit, I'm sorry. Sorry.

(Vic watches Darja holding her face, trying not to smile.)

But I'm not. I'm also not sorry. You got a good laugh.
Yo, lemme get you some ice. And a hotel. It's not terrible how
I got money. Not to me.

DARJA

Why you do what you do?

VIC

I like it.

DARJA

You like doing what you do to people?

VIC

Wouldn't do it if I didn't.

DARJA

But . . . you are hurting people.

VIC

I mean, only if they're *into* that, nam'sayin. I ain't tryin to *force*
nobody to come to me. And it's good conversation sometimes
too. Before, y'know. Before it gets goin. Sometimes I'm like shit,
should I pay *you*?

Yeah, man. I like it.
. . .
So what's up, you wanna go?

DARJA

You must really need this money if—

VIC

I don't. Okay? Truth is, these men *think* they need to pay me. I think they feel better payin, after. And, so, that's cool. Whatever. That's cool.

DARJA

Men?

VIC

Yeah. Men. What.
Don't tell nobody. Okay?
It ain't about money for me. And anyway I don't like bein home either so.

DARJA

Why you don't like?

VIC

Yo, you hungry? Wanna hit up a diner?

DARJA

Why you—

VIC

Look, it's not like *your* situation or anything, my house?, but I mean . . . it's a different kinda shitty situation but it ain't no better than yours.

I mean.
Shit.
I mean, it's *prob'ly* better than yours but.
There's just something very wrong there. At my house.
And if they *really*, y'know, knew about me . . .

85

So. Tops? Tick Tock? Yo, or we could just walk to Olympia from here.

DARJA

What these places are?

VIC

Diners.

DARJA

I never been these places.

VIC

What. You. What. You live in Jersey, right?

DARJA

Yes.

VIC

And you never been to a diner?

DARJA

No.

VIC

GIRL. There's like a third of the country's diners in Jersey and that is a FACT. Babies come out the womb suckin on Disco Fries. You seriously never been?

DARJA

Is just food, yes?

VIC

"Just" . . . okay. You need to come with me right now. This is real.

(She's not moving.)

I got this.

DARJA

And then we go to hotel?

VIC

Yeah.
I mean NO.
I mean nah.
I mean *you* can stay at the hotel. I'll crash maybe but that's all.
I got school tomorrow.

DARJA

School?

VIC

High. High school. In the morning.

DARJA

You?

VIC

I look mad mature.

DARJA

You go to high school?

VIC

Most days, yeah.

DARJA

You know my son?

VIC

Oh shit do I? What grade he in?

DARJA

Freshman.

87

VIC

Oh word? I'm a junior.
Where he go?
Cuz uh I'm at Seton Hall Prep.

*(He fishes under his shirt. Whips out a tie.
Hangs it over his baggy shirt like a tongue.)*

I'ma guess he ain't at Seton Hall Prep, is he?

DARJA

You are rich?

VIC

So don't feel bad.

Cmon, some people were supposed to come get me. Not the first
time they ditched me so. Whatever, y'know. I kinda got nowhere
to go.

DARJA

You got home to go.

VIC

You don't wanna hang?

DARJA

What?

VIC

Spend time? Together?

DARJA

I'm thirty-four-years-old woman.

VIC

So?

DARJA

So you don't want to be spending your time with me.

VIC

You don't like my company?

. . .

DARJA

(The truth) I . . . I am so tired.

VIC

Arright, man, so I'll just take you to a hotel. You can sleep. Call yer son.

DARJA

He's at friend's house.

VIC

Must be nice.
Friend's house.

DARJA

No. No they are not.
No.

. . .

VIC

He can come too.
To the hotel.
I mean, if he cute.
. . .
Did uh . . . did stuff happen to him too? To yer son? Tonight?

(She looks away.)

Yeah you ain't goin home tonight.

DARJA

No I should go. I don't even know what time it's—

VIC

It's late. Cmon. They got ice in hotels. You ever been in one?

DARJA

I clean *houses*. Not hotels.

VIC

I think you'll like it.

Or we can just go to my house. I can get us a cab. House is so big no one's even gonna know yer there. You can just crash. Sleep. Eat some breakfast. YO. I make baller fuckin pancakes. Blueberry 'n' shit.

DARJA

I don't know I should go—

VIC

Okay. Yer skeeved. Understandable. You don't know me. Look, I'ma just give you the money. We'll get you a hotel. And I'll walk you there. I can even drop you off like a block away if you want. I don't hafta stay if yer not good with it.

Or, here. Why don't you just, here.

(Vic takes out a wad of cash. Extends it to Darja.
Darja looks at Vic a long moment. Considering.)

For real. It's cool.

(Suddenly, Darja embraces him to her, strong.
He's taken aback.
But sinks into it. We see his need here too.)

It's cool, man. No bigs.

DARJA

I can't take it.

VIC

I'm sure you can, man. Look, I was gonna pay for a hotel tonight anyway. Guys from school they can't like, toke at home obviously so. I know they only call me up so I can bankroll that shit for em. I usually just sit in the corner while they smoke and like, feel girls up 'n' shit. Most times they're too fucked up to even say Thank You.

It's just like a hundred bucks. Seriously, it's just pocket money. It's just money.
You can have it.

DARJA

I can't.

VIC

Why?

(A car passes. It blares its horns.
Vic and Darja separate.)

Oh, shit.
Oh shit that's them.
They
shit wow
they actually showed.

DARJA

You should go.

VIC

Nah, man.
. . .
(Tempted) Should I?

DARJA

You want to?

VIC

Can I?

. . .

DARJA

Yes.
Go.

VIC

You sure?

DARJA

I know you want to.
Be careful.
(Genuine) Have fun.

VIC

'Ey but, here, man.

(Vic tries to give her the money.)

DARJA

No. I can't take nothing from you.

VIC

Yeah you can.

DARJA

Is okay, I can sleep behind factory—

VIC

Take it.

DARJA

—or maybe I go to diner, stay there what it's left of the night.

VIC

Just take it. They're turnin the car around.

DARJA

So you will need this for tonight.

VIC

Take it.

DARJA

No.

VIC

Cmon, I gotta go.

DARJA

No.

VIC

Give it to yer son then.

(Car horn.)

DARJA

You think this can do something?, this hundred dollars?

VIC

What?

DARJA

I sleep one night in hotel and then I what? One night I sleep and then, next day, I what?

Or I go get my son, we sleep or we take bus some place and then
we what? Everything will just okay?

I take care myself my son.
But *I* do this.
Don't give to me money you feel bad my son.

VIC

Yo I'm just tryin to help.

DARJA

Don't give to me money so you don't feel bad.

(Car horn.)

VIC

Don't fuck him over so *you* don't feel bad.

(Car horn.)

DARJA

They will not wait so long. Go. Your friends are waiting.

VIC

Yo, if I throw this on the ground, will you take it or you gonna let
it roll away?

(Car engine. Vic looks toward it. Back at Darja.)

Look over there.

DARJA

What?

VIC

Look over there. That way.

(Vic points in the opposite direction of the car of friends.)

DARJA

(Knows what he's doing) No.

VIC

Just, cmon, man, look over there.
"Oh shit!
Look at that moon!"
Wow.

(She hesitates.
She knows what Vic will do.
But she does. She looks at the moon.
They both look at the moon a moment.
. . .
Then, simultaneously, Darja extends her hand, softly,
and Vic, also softly, slips some money into her hand.
A handoff, of sorts.
All while still looking at the moon.
They squeeze hands as a goodbye.
But never look each other in the eyes.
Then Vic runs away, toward the car.
It drives off.
Darja, alone.
She looks down at the money in her hands.
Looks back after Vic, now gone.
And holds this stranger in her heart for a moment.
She remembers the money.
She considers.
Decides.
And takes out her phone.)

DARJA

Halo, kochanie. Is me. Your mom.
I'm okay.

I hope you okay.
Wherever you go.
Tonight.
I know where you go and I don't like it.
Call me back.

(She hangs up.
Considers.
Calls back.)

Halo. Kochanie.
Don't go home tomorrow.
Tomorrow, am cleaning house in Montclair.
They won't be there so after school I want you take bus to Montclair. Meet me there.
Don't go home.
We figure out what we will do.
Don't go home.
We will not go home.
Okay.
Am going to diner now.
Call me back.

(She hangs up.
Considers leaving.
Something stops her.
. . .
She calls again.)

Halo.
Aleks.
Kochanie.
It's me. Your mom.
I am so fucking sorry.
. . .
("Bye") Okay.

(She hangs up.
She knows he won't call back.
She looks up at the sky. Dawn.
She blows out her candle.
Sits and considers just waiting here until morning.
. . .
Darja's phone rings.
She sees who's calling.
She picks it up, hurriedly.)

Aleks?

Aleks!

Scene Five: 2014. Winter.

The thaw.
Early morning, where it still looks like night.
Darja holds her phone in her hands.
Tommy enters. He's better put together than we've seen him. He's trying.
He fixes his hair with his palm. He carries flowers wrapped in plastic,
bought at a gas station on the way here.
Tommy has thought about what he'd say for the past few hours.

TOMMY
Before you say anything . . . Okay, before you say anything, just lemme say:
(*Nerves*) Woo. Okay.
OKAY.

I just wanna, lemme just say, I know it's been a few days. I know we haven't talked in a few days so lemme just start with, lemme just say:

I'm sorry.
You can come back home.
No charge.

I could just take you home. Right now. You can quit wastin money at motels and hostel whatevers. And you can borrow my car. Any time. Where you goin? You goin to work? You get a job? Goin to work? Wanna borrow my car? You *want* my car? Shit, I can even start takin the *bus*. Try *that* out.

I got you flowers.

DARJA

Did her husband find out?

TOMMY

What?

DARJA

Is this why she leave you?

TOMMY

What're you talkin about?

DARJA

Linda's husband. Did he find out and so you are alone now? With space in the apartment? Time to buy flowers?

. . .
. . .
. . .

TOMMY

Will you marry me.
. . .

So I um I don't got a ring. There's a funny story actually for why no ring. But I *was* gonna do um—cuz I don't want you thinkin I didn't like, *plan*. See, I was gonna, see—

(Tommy points his key fob at an offstage car.
Beep-Beep.
Headlights.
Then, static-y Springsteen . . .
The intro to "Secret Garden" from the soundtrack to Jerry Maguire.*)*

Bruce.
Only the best for my baby.

(They listen.
Tommy, totally into it.
Darja, not so much.
Perhaps he inches closer to her.
Perhaps he takes her hand. Or tries to.
They stare ahead.
They listen to the song and stand awkwardly for a long time.)

. . .

Will you marry me?

. . .

(They listen to Bruce.)

. . .

DARJA

My husband died.

TOMMY

What?

DARJA

Maks.

(Tommy turns off the Bruce.)

My first husband.
Aleks's father.
He died.
Last night.
Aleks called me.
He it's in Chicago.
With my car.
They, apparently, he and my car and Maks, they all are in Chicago.
That's where he go.
To Maks.
Before he—
To meet him.

TOMMY

What happened? To . . .

DARJA

He was sick.

TOMMY

But what . . . happened?

DARJA

. . . He got sick.

TOMMY

Holy fuck. Holy fuck, I'm so sorry. Were you close?

DARJA

What?

TOMMY

Sorry that's, that's a stupid fuckin.
Fuck. Darja.
I'm sorry.

. . .

What time's yer flight?

DARJA

Flight?

TOMMY

To Chicago. You want a ride?, to the airport?

DARJA

I don't have flight.

TOMMY

So why're you here?, at the bus stop?

DARJA

I just, I just come here.
I don't know why.
This is just what I do.

. . .

I want to go.

TOMMY

I can take you.

DARJA

No.

TOMMY

I can help you.

DARJA

No, Tommy.

TOMMY

I can lend you the money. For a ticket.
It's no problem.
But. . .
But I could also just buy it.

(Darja considers.)

Don't be stubborn, D.
Funerals happen once. And fast.
. . .
I'll buy it.
Okay?

DARJA

Fuck. I hate this.

TOMMY

It's okay.

DARJA

I don't want to be like this.

TOMMY

It's okay.

DARJA

Your insurance it's still Blue Cross Blue Shield?

. . .

TOMMY

Are you serious?

DARJA

Yes.

TOMMY

For Aleks?

. . .

DARJA

(A rare nervousness) Yes.

. . .
. . .

TOMMY

There's co-pays.

DARJA

I can co-pay.

TOMMY

And he can only use it til he's twenty-six. After that, good luck.

DARJA

That's four years. That's good. In four years, many things can change.

TOMMY

And I dunno if rehab's covered.

DARJA

Better than nothing.

TOMMY

You think he cares about you this way?

DARJA

What?

TOMMY

You think your son would ever take care of you?

DARJA

I don't do this so he can pay me back.

TOMMY

So why then? Why all the time Aleks? How come he can——? And you still . . . how come?

DARJA

You would not know how to understand this.

TOMMY

Then it doesn't exist. Everyone's capable of understandin everything. We got all the same parts. You just gotta put it in my terms.

DARJA

You would not understand.

TOMMY

You want health insurance?

DARJA

You want woman what don't leave you?

TOMMY

Sounds like there's no guarantee of that, is there.

DARJA

And it's no guarantee your Blue Cross can do anything but what I can do but try? I am not this kind of person what sits and thinks Why whole the time. He it's my son. He can do every horrible thing to me and I will look to him and say This is Mine. This is what I have in whole this world what's mine. You have your love

and you give to everybody. This world it have millions peoples
like me, millions womens. But is only one me for him. He can't to
throw this away.

TOMMY

Billions.

DARJA

What?

TOMMY

Billions of women, actually. There are actually billions of women
out there. You said millions but—it's billions.
I was just doin that thing where I listen real well.
Billions. Just like you. To choose from.
But you see what I'm doin here?

(He gets down on one knee.)

I don't have a ring but do you see what I'm doin? Look, I'm not
a fuckin stud, okay. I know that. I'm arright. But listen. And no
I don't exactly make bank. But I pay my bills. And yeah I've fucked
up. Fucked around. Okay. But yer also not a model sorry and I still
love the fuckin shit outta you. Yer logic's aggravation, yer English is ridiculous, and you are one straight-up crazy fuckin—yer
crazy, D, sometimes. But you got wonderful legs. And yer heart
is good. You like goin to the movies. I LOVE goin to the movies.
You need a car. I got a car. I can make you pasta. You could make
me lunches. And it's good to know that someone's got the keys
if I forget mine.

Darja. Aleks didn't get to choose.
And he hasn't. He hasn't been. Choosin. Lately. You.
I do.
And I will. Every day. Fuckin swear.

. . .

Yes?

. . .

No?

. . .

. . .

Okay.

(Tommy gets off his knee.)

Okay. Okay, I'll just drop it. I guess you can forget it. Sorry. I don't
even have a ring. Not even a fuckin silver one.

(The stores don't open—I just wanna say—not this early.)

. . .

I knew Linda would leave. I think. In my like, heart.
They always leave. Allison. Courtney. All of em. Eventually.
I mean . . . stay. They never leave. They just stay where they always
been and I gotta leave.
I go home.
But now yer not there.
And it's so— . . .

At least you tap my phone.
Which is fucked but.
At least you gave a fuck enough about me to tap my phone.
Which is something.

You know my mother's birthday.
Backwards.
Which is something.

I knew you'd be here.
I knew that.
Which, I think,
is something.

. . .

(Dropping it) Okay.

(Tommy moves to exit.)

DARJA

Bruce was nice.

TOMMY

Yeah?

. . .

. . . Will you marry me?

. . .

DARJA

Probably.

TOMMY

(Spiking the flowers) YES.

DARJA

But wait. Wait. Talk to me like, terms. So you would give insurance, rent—

TOMMY

Half the rent once you get on yer feet.

DARJA

Okay—

TOMMY

And I'll make pasta sometimes.

DARJA

(He makes shitty pasta) Okay. Insurance, half the rent. And then what you want?

TOMMY

A marriage.

DARJA

Yeah okay but I asking what you want. I get insurance and you get someone to come home to. What does not tap your phone. Unless you like that.

And— . . .

TOMMY

And . . . Aleks?

. . .

DARJA

And . . . Aleks . . . would not have to live with us.
He can live close, very close, but he would not have to live with us.

TOMMY

It's okay, we can // talk about—

DARJA

He does not *have* to live with us.
But he might. Or close.
So, okay, so all this and then you do whatever?

TOMMY

That's not a marriage, just doin whatever.

DARJA

Okay, you are never married.
Just maybe we can get all this in writing? That we will try to be
nice like this to each other.

TOMMY

If we get married, that's pretty much what we're fuckin doin. Listen, I'm gonna get the car right now and drive you to the airport.
This bus shit?: aggravation.

DARJA

You are never married and you never ride this bus. You don't
know what's aggravation.

TOMMY

I never rode this bus cuz I never had to.

DARJA

No. No one rides this they don't have to.

TOMMY

You don't have to.

DARJA

I have to.

TOMMY

Aggravation! I'm gettin the car.

(Heads off.)

DARJA

Tommy.
But what this is? What would be deal?

(He turns back.)

TOMMY

You do things for me. I do things for you. Marriage. Like right now, I'm about to get the car and pull up and get you like it's my fuckin job. Right up to your toes. Without you even askin.

DARJA

And later I do things for you.

TOMMY

Maybe.
If you want.

(Darja considers.)

Can I come?

DARJA

Where?

TOMMY

To Chicago?
Can I take you?
We can drive.

. . .

DARJA

I did not say yes yet.

TOMMY

I know.

DARJA

So don't try to be sneaky-charming, okay. Because everything it's not all fixed.

TOMMY

I know.

DARJA

"Probably" means maybe and not yes.

TOMMY

Okay.

DARJA

I can't answer now this, your, I can't answer right now your, question.

TOMMY

Okay.

DARJA

And I will drive.

. . .

TOMMY

(She's a shitty driver) Okay.

. . .

DARJA

We maybe figure something out.
Maybe.
We'll // see—

(Tommy's cell phone rings.
He freezes.
Ring.
. . .

Tommy turns off the phone in his pocket, without even looking to see who is calling.
. . .
Darja remembers and guards herself.)

Get the car.

(Tommy exits.
Darja stands alone, hesitant to move.
She turns to go, but—
Maks enters from another part of the stage.
We're in the 1990s for a moment.
He goes to stand with Darja.)

                         MAKS
Five minutes.
Last chance.
We are here waiting already two hours. After this, it's no more buses left.

. . .

Four minutes.

                         DARJA
No, Maks.

                         MAKS
Why no?

                         DARJA
Because I have already job.

                         MAKS
In shit factory.

DARJA

Yes.
In shit factory.

MAKS

It's shit factories in Chicago. Jobs, many kinds jobs, in Chicago.
There it's prob'ly five already waits for me. For you too can be, if
// you—

DARJA

I have job.
In New Jersey.
Right there. *(Indicates factory)*

MAKS

He it's picking you up?

DARJA

What?

MAKS

After I go? With car?

DARJA

Who?

MAKS

Nice car?
I see him talking with you this week. The boss.
He picks you up? Hm? Takes you home?

DARJA

No.
(A dig) Am taking *bus.*
And so what we talk?
He likes me. I'm great person.

MAKS

Even with little Maks he likes you?
Wow. What a guy.
He knows, in few months, you will have . . .
little . . . ?

DARJA

Nothing it's going on with me and the— And if this it's all you
think about this moment, then you got a big problem, Maks, what
things you think about.

(Not warm) I hope Chicago will not be too cold for you.

. . .

. . .

MAKS

Just come. I still can buy for you ticket. Just come and, and you
see how you like.

DARJA

Things there it's so different really?

MAKS

Yes. Yes! There, it's, in Chicago, it's—

DARJA

You would be different?

. . .

You would want what I want?

This it's not I like one place this world or some other place. Chicago or— There it's life already here, Maks. I follow you this
country. This it's enough far for me—

MAKS

Okay so just one more time you come with // me—

DARJA

No, maybe now you follow me. And stay.

MAKS

Darju, this is last one. Last bus. I can't use tomorrow my ticket. They don't give me money back.

DARJA

So? It's just money.

MAKS

It's not just—

DARJA

You can burn money. Gone, two seconds. Money it's nothing.

MAKS

Money's it's not nothing and you know this. This has to be today. We can talk forever this and nothing will happen, we just will be standing here.
I want this more than anything my life, how you can't see this?

(She looks at him.
And she does.
She does see this.
And makes the decision to let him go.)

DARJA

You speaking English.

MAKS

I know. I practice all the fucking time.

DARJA

Is nice.
Is good.
You will go far.

(Headlights.
The last bus is coming.
They watch it approaching.)

MAKS

I can send you money.

DARJA

I can send *you* money. I work harder.

MAKS

(Tries to give her money) Here, // take this, it's all I have—

DARJA

No!, go. No! Maks, I don't want—

MAKS

Take it. So you can buy ticket.

DARJA

No.

MAKS

Then—sing.

DARJA

What? // No.

MAKS

Sing with me. One time.

DARJA

Your bus—

MAKS

Just one time you sing with me. Then
you and
you and
you go have good life.

And you will have nice thing of me for remembering.
I would like my home in your mind to be nice place.

(Darja considers.
Then, the sound of the bus readying to depart.
They look toward it.)

DARJA

Go. It's going, go.

MAKS

Darju—

DARJA

Go!

(Maks and Darja quickly and achingly say goodbye without words.
There's no time.
Maks runs after the bus.
Maks is gone.
Darja watches him leave.
Darja watches Maks in the bus, leaving forever.)

Nie idź! Proszę cię. Ja nie mogę. Nie mogę sama. Sama nie mogę.
Kochanie . . .

(Harmonica. Maks appears somewhere else in space and time.
Somewhere in a different, rewritten reality.
Maks plays.
"Sittin' on Top of the World" by Howlin' Wolf.
The stage falls away.
The smog falls away.
What was once a bruised black backdrop becomes a sky full of stars.
A huge moon.
A beautiful night.

Maks plays.
It's wonderful.

Darja opens her mouth to sing.
Then:

Beep-Beep. Car horn.

The stage returns to how we've seen it.
2014.
Maks is gone.
The stars are gone.

. . .

Darja stands alone in the quiet of the present.

. . .
. . .

Car horn.
Darja looks toward it.
And begins to walk toward the car.
Then, stops a moment.

Darja sings for herself.

It's lovely
quiet
small
and entirely un-virtuosic.)

(Singing) fuck this bus . . .
oh yeah . . .
fuck this bus . . .

. . .

(She looks at where she is.
She looks at what was.

. . .

She looks at where she is.

. . .
. . .

She exits.

. . .

Dawn.
A bus stop stands alone.
A day begins.)

END OF PLAY

Sanctuary City

ANNA

And poor Katey when you're away? What
does she do?

(Anna looks at Kate.)

KATE

Oh, I continue.

—HAROLD PINTER, *OLD TIMES*

G (Sharlene Cruz) and B (Jasai Chase-Owens) in the New York Theatre Workshop production. Photo: Joan Marcus.

Production History

Sanctuary City had its world premiere at New York Theatre Workshop (James C. Nicola, Artistic Director; Jeremy Blocker, Managing Director) on September 21, 2021. It was directed by Rebecca Frecknall, with Caitlin Sullivan serving as the remount director. The scenic and costume design were by Tom Scutt, the lighting design was by Isabella Byrd, the sound design was by Mikaal Sulaiman; the production stage manager was Merrick A. B. Williams. The cast was:

B	Jasai Chase-Owens
G	Sharlene Cruz
HENRY	Austin Smith, Julian Elijah Martinez

PEOPLE

G, female, ages seventeen to twenty-one
B, male, ages seventeen to twenty-one
HENRY, male, older

G and B were born in other countries and brought to America young. Henry is first generation. Born in America of immigrant parents. All have American mouths. All were raised working class.

PLACE

Newark, New Jersey, and thereabouts.
2001–2006.

A bare stage. And then, perhaps, a surprise.

DIALOGISTICS

Slashes // indicate overlap.
Ellipses . . . are active silences.
[Square brackets] are words intended but unspoken.
(Non-italicized parentheses) within dialogue are meant to be spoken.

* * *
* * *

indicates a new memory.

NOTES

The countries of origin can suit the actors chosen. No character, however, is of Western European origin/ethnicity, or from a country of greater liberalism than the United States, especially as it relates to marriage equality in 2006 or earlier. These characters have grown up within working-class, multicultural America. They have connections, feelings, and knowledge of their countries of origin (or, in Henry's case, the country of his parents), but I limited moments of this in the script in an effort to encourage wider, more inclusive casting across subsequent productions, which need not replicate the casting of the original production. I hope this translates to more opportunities for actors from various backgrounds—as well as more opportunities for, and versions of, this story. In the original production at New York Theatre Workshop, G was Dominican, B was Haitian, and Henry was of Ghanaian descent. But G or B or Henry can be Vietnamese, Pakistani, Ecuadorian, Uzbek, Uighur, Eritrean, Brazilian—just some amongst many options and possibilities. I invite you to use this play to mindfully reflect the realities of your community, as it relates to class and immigration. B wants to stay in America because this is where he's made his life, not because he isn't proud of or does not love where he comes from. He feels his home to be here, as well as the specific future he imagines for himself.

There are no props or mime in the first part of the play beyond the two objects specified.

Avoid sentimentality and self-pity. They have no currency in these characters' world.

These characters are fighting this hard because they love this hard. Moments of cruelty and possession are born from the intense fear of losing their safest home in this world—each other.

```
*   *   *
*   *   *
```

Knock knock knock on a window. Late night. Winter 2001.

G

Can you let me in

B

You climbed up the fire escape?

G

Can I come in

B

What time is You know I have a test // tomorrow—

G

Open the window

129

B
(Continuing) —first period—

G
Quick before someone calls the cops

B
No one's gonna No one ever calls the // cops

G
Or just come downstairs and // let me in

B
Hold on

G
It's freezing

B
Hold on

G
It's freezing

B
HOLD—

(Window's open.)

G
I didn't wanna wake yer mom, buzz the

B
It's freezing

G
(Continuing) so I climbed up the

B

Where's yer coat?

G

I know it's late

B

Where's yer coat? It's freezing.
Fuck it's freezing.

G

I know.

(He sees her.
He knows.

A gust of wind.)

B

What happened.

. . .

G

Can you close the window.

* * *
* * *

Knock knock knock on a window. Spring 2002.

B

She's goin back—

G

(Surprised to see him here) what the fuck

B

She's goin back!

G

What? Who— Hold on, manager's lookin at me.

B

I don't know what to do.

G

Just—meet me outside.

B

I don't know what to do.

* * *
* * *

B

What happened.

G

Can't wait to get away from—

B

Yer neck

G

—one day I'll—

B

Did you see yer neck?

G

It's at home.

B

What?

G

My coat.
Didn't have a chance to grab it.
Can you close the window?, My arm's *[hurt]*—I *[can't]*—

B

Yeah.

G

I never wanted to hurt someone so fuckin bad.
For him to hurt so fuckin
First opportunity I get, man, I'm outta there.

B

Is your mom okay?

. . .
. . .

G

Can I get under yer blanket real quick?

B

Yeah.

G

It's cold.

B

Better?

G

Yeah.

B

Good.

G

Can I crash with you tonight?

* * *
* * *

G

What happened.

B

She's goin back

G

Who?

B

Back home, my mom

G

// Back—?

B

(Coded shorthand of being in public; finality) She's goin back.

She's afraid of stayin in the country. There's some shit at work, she said. Boss keeps takin money from her tips cuz, y'know, he can. What's she gonna do?, report it?, to who? And she's afraid what happened to Jorge's gonna happen to her and so she's goin back.

And cuz of September.
Cuz of the towers.

G

keep yer voice they think i'm in the bathroom

B

(Referring to 9/11) Like—now anything can happen. Now anything
can happen here too now.
She didn't say that but
So she's goin back.

G

What about you?

B

She said I can decide.

G

Decide what.

B

If I wanna stay. // Or go back.

G

WHAT.

B

Yeah.

G

Did she give you a day—?

B

Like now Like she'd love to know right now. Soon. Real soon.
I'm seventeen, she says. Almost grown, she says. So she says I can
decide what I wanna do.

G

She didn't wanna wait til you finish school?

B

No.

G

But it's just one more year!

B

// No—

G

Yer senior year!

B

No she doesn't wanna wait.

I've been here ten years, man Ten years, we've been That's half my life More than half my I got everything here. Yeah, like, my family's there. But everything from over half my life?: that's all here.

G

Why would she just go—

B

I don't know what to do.

G

—without you?

B

. . .

G

She came here fer you. So why would she be goin back? Without you?
. . .
. . .
Did something happen?

. . .
. . .

B

I don't know what to do.

      * * *
      * * *

Late night. Quiet. In bed.

. . .
. . .
. . .

G

I got blood on yer sheets.

B

Oh—!

G

From my *arm.*
I'm sorry.

B

It's okay.

G

I'm sorry.

B

It's okay.
It's fine.

I'll say it's mine.

      * * *
      * * *

G

But then what're you gonna do about next year? Can you graduate?

B

If I stay.

G

What about college?

B

I can't go.

G

Why?!?

B

Unless I pay for it myself.
Which
I can't go.

* * *
* * *

B

What are you gonna say at school tomorrow?
About yer arm, yer neck—

G

I'm not goin.

B

Yeah.
Yeah prob'ly you should maybe don't.

* * *
* * *

B

What are you gonna say at school? About yer face—

G

I'm not goin.

B

Yeah.
Yeah prob'ly you should maybe don't.

* * *
* * *

B

What are you gonna say at school? About yer eye—

G

I'm not goin.

B

Yeah.

* * *
* * *

B

What are you gonna say at school? About—

G

I'm not goin.

B

Yeah.
Yeah prob'ly you should maybe // don't.

G

Last time this shit happened, (remember?, my eye?), Miss Romano
saw, sent me to the nurse, nurse called my mom, Mom said I fell,
then she freaked the fuck out on me when I came home. She said
to say I fuckin fell, whatever. Said to say I always fall, I fell.
Which I think they'll buy once.

B

I can bring you the homework.

G

Say I'm sick.

B

The flu?

* * *
* * *

B

I can bring you the homework.

G

Say I'm sick.

B

The flu.

G

Used flu last time.

B

A cold?

G

Yeah just say a cold.

* * *
* * *

. . .
. . .

                    B

I'll bring you the homework.

. . .

                    G

(Not looking at him) say i'm sick

                    B

A cold?

                    G

something longer

                    B

Right.

                    G

(Continuing) need a few days this time

. . .

                    B

Chicken pox?

. . .

                    G

yeah
say chicken pox

MARTYNA MAJOK

* * *
* * *

B

I can bring you the homework.

G

Say I'm sick.

B

Chicken // pox.

G

Used that already.

B

Right. Measles?

G

("No") Mm.

B

Mumps.

G

The fuck's mumps?

B

Stomach bug.

G

No.

B

Why.

G

Cuz no that's nasty no.

B

Lice.

G

NO.

B

Crabs.

(She is not amused.
He is.)

A cold.

G

Yeah I think it's fine to use a cold again.

B

A cold.

G

A bad one.

B

A really bad // cold.

G

DON'T SAY LICE.

* * *
* * *

B

I can bring you the homework.

G

Say I'm sick. The flu.

. . .

B

Are you sure you don't just wanna tell // somebody—?

G

(Finality) No.
She's scared they'll send us back if they find out what's goin on at
home.

B

Who?

G

(Continuing) Or just her.
She's scared they'd separate us.

B

Who would send you back?

G

America. If they wanted to investigate. If they like—checked. She
worked with a fake social security for years. He's threatened to
report her before. Everyone's more, y'know—*[careful / nervous]*

B

Yeah.

G

—cuz of September. Cuz of the towers.

Or maybe they'd put me in some kind of—some place for kids—
separate us. I don't know if she even knows specifically what to
be afraid of but she is. She's scared. There's that place on Fish Kill
Road. In South Kearny. The place Rogelio's dad got sent to.

B

That's just for guys, that place, // I think.

G

I don't wanna get separated. Or for her to go to Fish Kill Road.

B

It's just for guys.

G

So where do they send women? They gotta have somewhere to
put the women. Where's the women go?

B

I don't know.
Further away.
I guess.

. . .

G

I don't wanna get separated.
I don't want anything like
Like Fish Kill
I know there's people Even if it's just for guys
I know there's people there on Fish Kill Road.
Behind wire.
I see them. We drive by and I see.
There's barbed wire and people and I don't wanna go.

B

You wouldn't hafta go—

G

That place is real.
It's just better not to talk about anything that happens at home.
Better I say I fell.
Or have the flu.

B

Maybe it would be good to be separated.

G

Not from my mom.

B

No but—

G

(Firm finality) She's never gonna leave him. You think I haven't asked?

I asked.
. . .
You want me to hide under yer bed?, from yer mom—

B

It's okay.

G

(Continuing) Or I can just jet right now. Before she wakes up. If you need me out.

B

It's okay, my mom won't care.

G

(Continuing) I'll just walk around the neighborhood. Go to Tops. Hang out there. Eat some eggs. I didn't finish the math anyway.

B

You can just stay here.

G

I've been comin by a lot.

B

So stay. Eat breakfast with us.

G

You eat breakfast?

B

Not usually but. I could.

. . .

G

Yeah?

B

We could. Together, yeah. I got eggs.
Stay.

* * *
* * *

G

Don't go.

B

Then I'd end up just like her. If I stay in the country, I'd be just
like my mom, doin whatever job—shitty job—whatever shitty
job would take her just to fuck her over down the line.

G

But you went to school—

B

(*Continuing*) Always scared.

G

You did like, all of school here.

B

Doesn't matter. My mom brought me over. And she kept me over.

G

So?

B

So when she overstayed her visa, so did I.

G

But you were a kid.

B

We were supposed to go back nine years ago.

G

And you were supposed to know that? You were supposed to buy a plane ticket? At fuckin, eight?—

B

Doesn't matter.

G

You were a kid.

B

It doesn't matter. If they find out how long we've been here, we won't even be allowed back for another ten fuckin years.

G

Don't go.

```
*  *  *
*  *  *
```

The urban version of crickets.

. . .

. . .

G

Yer mom's gonna think we're sleepin together.

B

We are sleepin together.

G

I mean like, together.

B

I don't think so.

. . .

G

WHY THE FUCK NOT.

```
*  *  *
*  *  *
```

B

Which
I can't go.

G

But why?

B

Cuz I can't pay for that! For college? By myself?

G

Neither can I but—aid.

B

I can't apply for aid.

G

Why.

B

CUZ I'M NOT SUPPOSED TO BE HERE.

. . .

. . .

G

okay wow cuz I never scream at you when you ask me // questions

B

We came here legal but we didn't stay here legal. We overstayed.
So I'm a fuckin criminal, according to Here. I could pay for school.
If I *could* pay for school. They'd like, take my money—if I *had*—
like, happily Listen I could do a lotta things if I had money.

(Finality) I can't get aid. Can't apply for federal financial aid. Can't
go.

G

Yer mom can't help?

B

(Firm finality) My mom is leaving

. . .

. . .

G

What about community college?—

B

No.

G

But you could // still—

B

No fuck that you know how fuckin hard I worked since comin here fuck that.
I get better grades than fuckin, everyone in there.
I work harder than
Fuck that.

* * *
* * *

G

G'night.

B

G'night.

G

Hey.

B

Yeah?

G

Thank you.

B

No problem.

151

G
For real though. Thank you for lettin me stay.

B
It's okay.
G'night.

* * *
* * *

G
Hey.

B
Yeah?

G
Thanks.

B
All good.
G'night.

* * *
* * *

G
Hey—

B
(Impatient) Yeah?

. . .

G
(Quietly, feeling like a burden) thank you

. . .

B

(Truly) Any time.
Good night.

* * *
* * *

G

We'll find a way for you to stay.

B

There isn't one.

G

We'll make one.

B

I don't know if I can even Like how would I even My mother's workin a full-time job for this roof AND she has to borrow money from me sometimes. Comin home like, half-a-person, after work, exhausted. How'm I gonna do all that AND school? How'm I gonna do that?

G

You can live with me! At mine's!

B

You don't even wanna live at yours.

* * *
* * *

B

Good // night.

G

Hey.

153

B

Yeah?

G

Thanks.

B

(It is) It's okay.

       *   *   *
       *   *   *

G

Thank you.

B

(It is) It's okay.

       *   *   *
       *   *   *

G

Thank you.

B

(It is) It's okay.

G

I owe you.
Thank you.

. . .

(Nighttime.)

. . .
. . .

B
(In G's first language) Good night.

. . .

G
(In B's first language) Good night.

. . .

B & G
Good night.

* * *
* * *

G
I can help you pay rent!

B
What?

G
On this apartment. I'm over here all the time. We sort of kind of already live together here, sleep to—I sleep here sometimes. So I should help. I can pay.

B
Fer a year and then yer gone.

G
. . .

B
"First opportunity you get, man."

G

Just—finish school at least.

B

And then what?
Keep workin at the restaurant? Moppin floors? Washin dishes?
Go to war?
See if *they're* checkin papers.
Ship out with all the seniors still failin algebra.
Be like a fuckin, high school reunion—in Afghanistan.

. . .

G

We'll find a way for you to stay.

* * *
* * *

Knock knock knock on a door. Lost. Autumn 2002.

B

(Heartbroken) She left.

G

What?

B

She's gone.

* * *
* * *

Knock knock knock on a window. Found. Autumn 2002.

G

(Elated) We're leaving!

156

B

What?

G

She's gonna leave him! We're leaving!

* * *
* * *

B

And how're you gonna help me pay rent?

G

With my *job*.

B

And how much you make? Hundred a week?

G

Varies.

B

Can't bank on varies.

G

It varies but I'm there almost every day after school except
Thursdays.
Shit I've come away with a HUNDRED sometimes just on Fridays
cuz of tip-out.

B

Really?

G

Almost once yeah almost.
If things keep goin how they're goin at home, I'll be at yer place
a lot.

B

(Concern, not inconvenience) Really?

G

Unless you don't want me to.

B

No yer good.

G

Doesn't look like anything's gonna change. So I'll prob'ly be here
a lot.
If you'll like, have me.

. . .

B

I'll make you a key.

G

So I'll contribute.
That way, you won't hafta do this completely alone.
And you can finish school.

. . .

B

You sure?

G

Make me a key.

. . .
. . .

B

Yeah.
Yeah okay.
Yeah maybe I can do this—Yeah.

G

And you can rent out the extra room!

B

What room?

G

For extra money. You can rent out the extra room in this apartment!

B

. . .

G

When she. Eventually.

B

. . .

G

Sorry.

* * *
* * *

B

Yer leaving?

G

My mom 'n' I!

B

Where?

G

Schuyler Ave! Like right on the border! Close!

B

How did she——?

G

She got naturalized!

B

What?

G

She's a citizen now! She was takin all the tests, secret! She got a
naturalization certificate, a restraining order, and a fuckin moving
company, all secret! We're gonna, when he leaves for work, we're
gonna pack up all our shit and GO.

B

When?

G

Tomorrow morning. Today! In a few hours! TODAY! Movin guys
are comin soon as he's gone, then we gotta pack up everything we
can and haul that shit out fast. We gotta be outta there by four,
when he's back from work.
Back to an empty fuckin apartment!
She had this shit planned for months. *(Proud)* Fuckin, months!
I can't believe it. We're finally leaving! And I don't even hafta switch
schools!

B

(Something off) That's great.

G

I know!

B

Congratulations.
To yer mom.

G

We're both moving!

B

On becoming a citizen.

G

Oh and I'm one too!

B

What?

G

She snuck me in right under the deadline.

B

What do you—?

G

Right under the wire. Cuz if yer under eighteen, if the kid's under eighteen when the parent gets it, then it gets transferred to the kid. Automatic.

B

So you didn't hafta pay none of those fees?

G

Guess not!

B

Or hafta take the test?

G

Nope!

. . .

. . .

. . .

I'm sorry—

B

You gonna need help?
With packing?

G

We got the guys—

B

I know but do you need more help?
You gotta pack up an entire apartment in how long?

G

Yeah but it's during school.

B

So how are you gonna—

G

My mom's gonna call 'n' say I'm sick.
She planned that shit too!

B

So I'll say I'm sick.

G

No but you'd hafta miss school.

. . .

B

(He did) I didn't do the math anyway.

. . .

G

Okay.
Okay! Tomorrow, then.

B

You wanna crash here? Tonight?
One last time?

G

Why one last time?

. . .

(And she realizes.)

B

("Right," an end) I'll make eggs.

* * *
* * *

G

And you can rent out the extra room!

B

What room?

G

For extra money. You can rent out the extra room in this apartment!

B

...

G

When she. Eventually.

B

...

G

Sorry.

B

It's okay.

* * *
* * *

G

When?

B

(Heartbroken) This morning.

...
...

G

(Doesn't know what to say) . . . did she say goodbye to you?

B

(Not an answer to her question) I rode the train with her to the airport.
Helped carry her stuff.
They don't let you wait anymore. Did you know that?
They don't let you wait with yer person that's gonna board the
plane.

Cuz of September.
So if yer not gettin on a plane, they don't let you past security.
I watched it out the window.
Watched for hours.
Imagined her in one of em.
Knew she was in
one of em.
Flyin away.
. . .
. . .
. . .
fuckin, of course we said goodbye

G

sorry

B

We've been sayin goodbye since she bought the fuckin ticket.
You wanna crash?

G

Tonight?

B

With me? At mine's?

I don't wanna go back there.
By myself—

G

Yeah. // I can.

B

I know you got yer new place now.

G

I'd love to crash.

B

She left a glass of water on the table.
She drank out of it this morning and left it on the table.
It'll still be there.
There's gonna be parts of her all over the apartment.
Things she left. Clothes she wants me to donate.
I don't think I can . . .

G

It's okay.

B

Thanks.

G

It's okay.

* * *

* * *

B

There's so much to pack.

G

(Thrilled) There is
so much
to pack!

B

I mean you could just leave him a mess right? If there's shit you
don't want.

G

True.

B

(Continuing) Shit you don't wanna clean.

G

Yeah.

B

Yer never comin back so leave that Fuck a mess.

G

I thought about pissin in his bed.

B

Why don't you.

. . .

G

[Actually . . .]

B

[Just sayin . . .]

. . .

G

We'll see how we're doin on time.

*   *   *
*   *   *

B

(Heartbroken) Would you want any of em?

G

What.

B

Her clothes?

* * *
* * *

G

Let's start with the clothes.

B

(On a mission) Clothes.

G

I can do that if you wanna box the books.

B

(On a mission) Books.

G

I dunno how I coulda done this shit alone. Even with the guys.

B

[Gimme the] tape.
Yeah I dunno how you coulda either, those guys're garbage, get yer money back.

G

I'm gonna miss this place.

. . .

B

How could you miss this place?

G

Twelve years.

B

Yeah but.

G

Longer livin here than anywhere else.
Than
Longer than I known you even.

B

Still.

G

It's a place I was.
I'm *from* here.
Even though I was born in
I'm from *here*.
Wherever I end up endin up,
I'll have gotten there from this place. Here.
. . .
And it's closer to you than my new place is gonna be.

* * *
* * *

G

(Pissed) There's another one.

B

Another // what.

G

We JUST moved and there's already another guy. Like a weed.
Like a fuckin— At least he doesn't knock her unconscious—
YET—that I KNOW OF—YET— Just—
I dunno, man. I can't seem to keep a dick outta that woman.

. . .

B

That woman gave you life.

G

Yeah well so did yers and here we are.
Can I crash.

* * *
* * *

G

You still can't sleep?

B

. . .

G

Don't you have a test tomorrow? It's late.

B

(Quietly; lost) There's so much stuff. She left a life of stuff.

G

You don't hafta do this all right now. Come to bed.

B

Would you want any of em?

G

What?

B

Her clothes?
. . .
. . .
You don't have to // if—

G

No—just—you sure you don't wanna keep this?

B

If you like it, take it.

G

You sure?

B

Take it.

. . .

G

Thank you.

B

But don't throw it out okay. If you take it, don't just throw it out.

G

Okay.

B

Wear it.
Like, sometimes.

. . .

G

Come to bed.

* * *
* * *

G

Good // night.

B

Hey.

G

Yeah?

B

Thanks.

G

(It is) It's okay.

       * * *
       * * *

B

Thank you.

G

(It is) It's okay.

       * * *
       * * *

B

Thank you.
I owe you.

. . .

G

(It is) It's okay.

       * * *
       * * *

G

No fuckin way

B

Cmon

G

It's racist!

B

Not if I'm tellin you it's okay

G

This is so fucked up

B

So you'll do it?

G

No

B

Cmon!

G

Why can't you just write a note? I could forge a note.

B

Just be glad they don't want her to come in.
I'm calling.

G

No!

B

It's ringing

G

I'm not ready!

B

You've heard her talk enough // times—

G

This is so racist

B

(Continuing) —you've had like, nine years of research

G

This is so racist

B

It's ringing

G

This is so Hello!
(In B's mother's accent) Yes—hello! Good morning also to you.

B

(Quiet) yes!

(G is mortified.)

G

Yes Hello Yes, Um, So, My—son

B

(Quiet; finds this hilarious) oh my god

G

is sick.
The flu.

(B stifles laughter.
G sees this.)

No sorry.
Lice.
He is disgusting yes and cannot be in school Tell everyone Thank
you Bye.

*   *   *

*   *   *

B

What'd they feed you tonight?

G

Chicken Milanese.

B

Nice.

G

I brought some.

B

WHAT.

*   *   *

*   *   *

B

What'd they feed you tonight?

G

Penne vodka sauce.

B

YES.

* * *
* * *

B

What'd they feed you?

G

Penne vodka sauce.

B

YES.

G

With chicken.

B

YES FUCK YES.

* * *
* * *

B

What'd you get tonight?

G

Spaghetti.

B

Oh.
Okay.

* * *
* * *

B

What'd you get tonight?

G

Chicken—

B

YES.

* * *
* * *

B

What'd they give you? What'd you get tonight?

G

Actually so they want us to eat family meal at work now actually.

B

Oh.

G

Cuz people Yeah Cuz people take too much.

B

Sure.

G

Bring it home.
For their actual families.

B

Right.

G

You eat?

. . .

                    B
Yeah.

                              * * *
                              * * *

                    B
What's that?

                    G
Chicken // Milanese.

                    B
WHAT!

                              * * *
                              * * *

                    B
What'd they give you tonight?

                    G
Oh I'm so sorry. I forgot to grab food.

                    B
You didn't eat?

                    G
I forgot.

                    B
Oh.
Okay.
You hungry?

                    G
There might be somethin in the fridge.

B

Not much. Want me to run // to the store—

G

Why don't you check?

B

ShopRite's // open still—

G

Why don't you just check the fridge.

. . .

(B suspects something.)

. . .

Check the fridge.

. . .

(He looks at her, suspiciously . . .
. . . and moves to an unseen fridge.

He looks inside.

. . .

His face changes.

She lights a lighter.
This is the only time we see a physical object in this entire section.
It glows between them.)

(Singing) Happy Birthday to you, Happy Birthday to you, Happy—

(She sees his face.)

(Serious, grave) I'm sorry.
I meant it as a nice thing.

                                        B
(Resisting tears—of loneliness) I know.

. . .

                                        G
("For your loss," that she can't be here) I'm sorry.

                              * * *
                              * * *

                                        G
Where've you been?
It's three in the—

                                        B
(As he enters, passes her by, exits to bed) Out.

(A door shuts.)

. . .

                                        G
(Alone, sass) Okay.

                              * * *
                              * * *

                                        G
Where've you been—?

B

Good night Out Good night.

          * * *
          * * *

B

Where've you been?

G

Where've *you* been?

B

[Oh okay. You want a secret too.]

G

[Yeah, I want a secret too.]

B

(Sass) Okay.

G

(Sass) Okay.

          * * *
          * * *

B

Where've you been?

G

("Nowhere good") Can I get under yer blanket real quick.

B

Yeah.

G

It's cold.

. . .

B

Better?

G

Yeah.

. . .
. . .

(The feeling of home.)

Yeah.

B

Good.

* * *
* * *

Knock knock knock on a window. Spring 2003.

B

(Jumps, annoyed) jesus christ.

(Knock knock knock on a window.)

G

(Knocking) Can you open the // window?

B

the fuck—

G

(Knocking) Hello!

B

(To himself) are you fuckin kidding me right now

G

(Still knocking on window) What? I can't hear you!

B

I'm comin.

G

(Can't hear, still knocking) You gonna open the // window?

B

I'M COMIN AND I'M OPENIN IT NOW.

. . .

. . .

. . .

G

You mad?

B

I'm exhausted. These fuckin essays, fuckin, homework I'm just
not I'm not doin this fuckin math homework. Fuck math. Fuck all
of math. They called me into work tonight and what could I say.
Now it's two A.M. I'm so tired I don't even WHY DON'T YOU
JUST TAKE THE FUCKIN STAIRS.

G

Tradition.

B

You have the key.

G

I left it.
Can I crash?

B

I'm not doin well, you know.

G

Yer sick?

B

No. I'm // not—

G

What's wrong?

B

I'm tellin you. I'm not doin well. In school. I'm not doin well
with any of it. Work. I can't keep up. I'm so tired. I'm so Like It's
like I'm runnin in my sleep. Everywhere. All the time. Runnin.
Use the key. Please. Next time.

G

I got into school.

. . .

B

What.

G

I got // in—

B

Where.

G

. . . Boston.

. . .
. . .

B

Scholarship?

. . .
. . .
. . .

(Referring to what's in her bag) What's that?

G

A bottle.
The rest of a bottle.
To celebrate.

B

. . .

(G feels the absence of his joy for her. And she turns away from him.)

G

You can copy my math.

* * *
* * *

B

Check the fridge.

G

Why.

B
Why don't you just check the // fridge.

G
It's not my birthday // Why're you stealin my idea.

B
Just—
Check the fridge.

. . .

(She does, suspiciously.
Her face changes.)

There isn't a song for it but

Congratulations.
. . .
Oh no.

G
(Through tears—of appreciation) We clearly can't put shit in fridges!

B
No.

G
Thank you.

B
Congratulations.

. . .

G
("You have no idea how much") Thank you.

* * *
* * *

B

So you wanna go with me?

G

To the fuckin—?

B

Cmon!

G

("Lame") That shit's so—

B

What.

G

You like that shit?

B

You don't wanna dress up?

G

Isn't it like, seventy dollars? Don't they want like, seventy a head?

B

Yeah but.

G

And then I gotta buy a dress?

B

It doesn't hafta be expensive though.

G

A limo—

B

The bus, man, I dunno who you think I am.

G

And I gotta hang with these clowns all night?
For seventy dollars?

B

There'll be food!

G

For seventy dollars!?!
("No way") I dunno, man.
I dunno.

* * *
* * *

B

You look so good.

G

You look so good.

B

No you look so // good.

G

Shut the fuck up.

B

You do You look so good.

G

I'll punch you in the face.

B

I'd punch you in the face you'd still look good.

...

G

Where do I put this expensive-ass flower shit?

B

(Moved) You got me a—?

G

It's fuckin tradition.
You wanna do it yerself?

B

No you.

G

Okay how do I—?

B

I think you— Here, there's a—

G

Yeah

B

Just yeah pin it on my FUCK OW // FUCK

G

FUCK

                              B
TAKE IT OUT

                              G
FUCK

                          * * *
                          * * *

                              G
When did you meet?

                              B
Third grade.

                              G
What school?

                              B
Franklin.

                              G
Where was it located?

                              B
Hundred Davis.

                              G
In?

                              B
Kearny.

                              G
You went to a public school in Kearny but listed in your application your address during that time as being in Newark?

B

I lied. Gave a friend's address in Kearny. So I could go to the better school.

. . .

G

I don't know if you wanna tell em that.

B

You asked!

G

We'll hafta figure that one out.
Okay. Who was the teacher?

B

Which?, when?

G

Third grade, when we—

B

Miss Ramirez.

G

What color was her hair?

B

Gray.

G

What's the best pizza in town?

B

It asks that?

G

No but—

B

Can we skip to the harder ones?

G

We should start with the basics.

B

But we know this shit.

G

We should start with the basics.

* * *
* * *

B

I got you some flower shit too.

G

Aw.

B

Fer yer wrist.

G

Aw.

B

But now there's blood on the petals.
You wanna put it—?

G

No you. You put it. You Can Put It On My Wrist, Sir.
No wait!

B

What.

G

(Sly) Do it on the bus.

* * *
* * *

B

Just skip to the harder questions—

G

They could trick us.

B

How? All this shit is true. There's nothin to memorize. No new information.

G

What if you forget?

B

I'm not gonna forget where I went to school. Or where we met.

* * *
* * *

The recognizable beginnings of a corny song that was popular in 2003. Something like The Backstreet Boys' "I Want It That Way."

B and G enter prom.

G instantly sprouts a look of judgment and regret. She is above this. B is not.

He's kinda into it, in fact.

Then he sees G's face. Full of opinions and blame.

. . .

They stare out at prom.

. . .

Then B moves ever so slowly . . .

. . . til he's dancing.

G is mortified. Wants none of it. Nope. No thanks.

* * *
* * *

G

(Annoyed, challenging) Fine. What did the two of you have in common? Where did you go for dates? When did your relationship turn romantic? Wanna start there? When did your relationship turn romantic? Wanna start there?

* * *
* * *

A fun LOUD song that was popular in 2003. Something like OutKast's "Hey Ya!"
They're having a great time.

G

THIS IS THE WORST.

B

YEAH.

G

I HATE THIS.

B

I KNOW YOU DO.

G

I HATE THIS SO MUCH.

(She's having the greatest time.)

SPIN ME!

> * * *
> * * *

G

(Continued, still annoyed, challenging) Did your parents approve of the match? Why or why not? Have you ever had an argument that resulted in one of you sleepin in another room? Who, and which room?—

B

("Stop") Okay.

G

(Still annoyed) No where you wanna start Where do you wanna start You don't like how I started so where do you wanna start?

> * * *
> * * *

Distant popular music from 2003. Near the end of the night.
They are somewhere more secluded, apart from the rest of prom.
A slowness. They smoke. Smoke around them.
They stare forward.
They're connected enough to not need to look at each other.

. . .
. . .
. . .

G

He knew I was watchin.

. . .

(They stare ahead.)

. . .
. . .

There was this dog on my street.
My old street.
Neighbor's dog.
Big.
Ugly big.
Head like a fist.
A big gray fist.
In summers, they'd keep it chained out in front, to the fence,
while they were inside makin dinner—

B

How you know they were makin dinner?

G

You could hear the pots and pans from the street.
And everything else you could hear that too.
Which I guess meant people could hear everything that was goin
on in our place.
They could hear it from the street.
Which I guess meant nothing at all to people, I guess.

B

You want any of this?

G

("No") I'm good.

They kept the dog tied up outside cuz I guess it got in the way when they were makin dinner.

My stepfather would be comin back from work or from wherever, the bar, someone's stoop, and . . .

I think he knew I was watchin.

That from the window, I would watch him.

I think he knew cuz, on his way home, he'd stop at that dog.

He'd kneel down next to that dog.

And he would pet its big ugly head with the softest hands I ever seen.

He knew I was watchin.

He knew I was watchin him care for something.

That he had the capacity to be good to something.

That he was able to do that.

If that was what he wanted

I started a lot of the fights—

B

(Fact, not pandering/comforting) No you didn't.

G

Didn't stop em.

Didn't ignore him.

If I'd just kept my mouth shut and more often.

Prob'ly wasn't always worth The Last Word when the guy's got a hammer in his hand. Kitchen knife.

B

I got another bottle if you, in my jacket, // the pocket—

G

Nah.
Wait what kind.

B

Vodka.

G

Nah yeah I thought you might have something else.
Still got the vodka I DuckTaped to my leg.

B

That's gonna hurt later.

G

I shaved.

B

There are easier ways to do things.

. . .

(They stare out.)

. . .

. . .

. . .

G

It was worth it. I guess.
The seventy dollars.

(They stare out.)

B

That chicken parm.

G

Yeah that was bomb-ass chicken fuckin parm.

*(They stare out.
Smoke.)*

B

That cheese—

G

Hey.

B

Yeah.

G

Thank you.

B

It's okay.

G

Do you miss her?

. . .

. . .

B

I'll send her the pictures of us.
You in yer dress.

G

She prob'ly thinks we're sleepin together.

B

I don't think so.

. . .

G

What're you gonna do about next year?

B

Keep workin.

G

At the—

B

Yup. Pays. Close to home.
And they feed me after shifts.

G

Did you hear back? From any of the // schools—

B

(End of conversation) Can't afford it. Cmon let's go inside—

G

I wanna help you.

B

You can help me go inside.

G

I'm serious.
I wanna help you.
How can I help.

(A proposal) I'm a citizen now so.

(B realizes. Knows exactly what she means.)

B

. . .

G

How can I help.

* * *
* * *

G

(Still annoyed) Have you met each other's parents? How often do you see each other's parents? Where do they live? When was the last time you saw them? Where? For how long? What color are their kitchen curtains?—

B

Let's skip back.

G

Back to the——?, // uh-huh thought so.

B

The more basic ones, yeah.

G

Okay.
When did you meet?

B

Third grade.

G

What school?

B

Franklin.

G

Where was it located?

B

Hundred Davis.

G

In?

* * *
* * *

G

I'm serious.
I wanna help you.
How can I help.

* * *
* * *

Alone. Private. Quiet.

B

what time does your spouse arrive home from work
who takes care of payin the bills
do you have a joint bank account
where

* * *
* * *

G

(A proposal) I'm a citizen now so.

(B realizes. Knows exactly what she means.)

B

. . .

G

How can I help.

* * *
* * *

Alone. Private. Quiet.

                    B
what did the two of you have in common
who proposed to
did your parents approve of the
why or
when did your relationship turn romantic

            * * *
            * * *

The last song at prom. Something like K-Ci and JoJo's "All My Life."

. . .

(They dance.)

. . .
. . .

                    B
Hey.

                    G
I step on yer feet?

                    B
Hey.

                    G
Yeah.

B
(The biggest gift in the world) Thank you.

. . .

G
It's okay.

* * *
* * *

The late-night public transit bus ride home from prom. Enthusiastically drunk.

G
Oh shit are we on the Express?

B
"How many people attended the wedding?"

G
(Drunk-happy) Every people!

B
"Where was it held?"

G
Could we elope? // You wanna elope?

B
Oh shit could we elope?

G
I'd elope.

B

Then we wouldn't hafta feed people!
"Did you go on a honeymoon? // Where?"

G

Yeah, man, where we goin!

B

Are we really doin this?

G

I'm really doin this are you really doin this?

B

Cuz I'd really do this.

G

THEN LET'S REALLY DO // THIS.

B

("Not so loud") Okay. // It's late.

G

WE'RE REALLY GONNA DO THIS.

B

That man's starin at you.

G

I'M GETTING MARRIED STARE ALL YOU WANT.

B

He looks mad.

G

I CAN TAKE HIM.

* * *
* * *

G is over these questions. She knows this.

B

What size is your bed? Twin, // queen, or—?

G

Twin. But eventually queen.

B

Do you have a mattress, futon, or waterbed?

G

Waterbed, who wrote these? Yeah we have a twin // waterbed.

B

Who sleeps on each side of the—?

G

(Points to self) Left.
(Points to B) Right.

B

What form of contraception (birth control) // do you use?

G

I know what contraception // means.

B

I'm just reading what's there what's written there!

* * *
* * *

The quiet of task-doing.

B

Yer not gonna fold that?

G

I did fold that.

B

You just sorta rolled it.

G

That's folding.

B

You'll need warmer clothes than that.

G

They give you sweatshirts there.

B

You gotta buy those.

G

No everyone wears one they give you them.

. . .
. . .

(As if to self, not happy) There's so much to pack.

B

Can I keep this?

G

What.

No I'm takin that with me.

B

Can you bring it? When you come back? At break?
We're gonna need pictures. Proof. Of years together.

G

We can take more before I go. And at break.

B

You'll need to leave me some of your things.

G

What things?

B

For my room. In case of a home visit.
They surprise you sometimes, drop by where you live.

G

Home visit?

B

Yeah.

G

. . .

B

Just—leave me some like, personal things.
Things you'd leave at a—y'know. Makeup. Underwear.
An earring.

G

. . .

B

Just leave me something of yourself.

* * *
* * *

G

When was your wife's Oh Jesus when was your wife's last men-
strual period?

B

Yer gonna hafta make me a chart.

G

Have you ever had an argument that resulted in one of you sleep-
ing in another room?

B

. . .

G

Who, and which room?

B

. . .

G

Why?

* * *
* * *

B

Just leave me something of yourself.

* * *
* * *

G

Who, and which room?

B

...

G

Why?
What do you disagree about?

* * *
* * *

B

Just leave me something of yourself.
Before you go.

* * *
* * *

G

What do you disagree about?

* * *
* * *

B

Hey.

G

Yeah?

* * *
* * *

B

What do you disagree about?

* * *
* * *

G

Hey.

B

Yeah?

* * *
* * *

The bus stop. G keeps looking after the bus in nervous anticipation.

G

These bags, it's like I'm movin my whole life away.

B

Boston's not far.

G

Feels far, Boston.

B

You'll be back soon.

G

I'll be back in December.

B

Not Thanksgiving?

G

Depends.

B

Really?

G

Depends who she's got in that apartment with her, yeah.

B

Just come stay with me.
If you came down for Thanksgiving, we could just do it then.

G

I'll only have like, a day off—for—
I'll be back in December. At the latest. For winter break.
But we can call all the time. We'll talk all the time.

. . .

B

Are you nervous?
About . . . ?

G   B

School?   —the marriage?

. . .

(G looks at B.)

. . .
. . .

B

Don't be nervous.

G

I wish I'd flown.

B

Then we wouldn't get to say goodbye.
You know they don't let you wait anymore with yer—

G

(Sees bus approaching) Oh no!

> B

It's gonna be okay.

> G

I can still turn back.

> B

It's gonna be great.

> G

I don't wanna go. I don't wanna // get on this bus.

> B

You'll be back soon.

> G

(A threat, to someone offstage) HEY MAN.

> B

He's just // It's okay

> G

(A threat) HEY.

> B

(Continuing) He's just gonna put em under // the bus.

> G

WHAT IF THEY FALL OUT.

> B

They won't.

> G

WHAT IF SOMEONE TAKES MY SHIT.

B

I think you made it pretty clear to everyone on that bus they
shouldn't.

G

I don't like they took my bags.

B

It's okay.

G

(Continuing) I don't like any of this.

B

Hey.

G

(Continuing) I don't wanna—

B

Hey.

(He holds out a ring.
This is the only other time we see a physical object in this section.)

. . .
. . .
. . .

G

. . . where did you . . .

B

My mom left it for me.
In case.

. . .
. . .

(Carefully and respectfully, he takes her hands.
Is this the kindest way a man has ever touched her hand?
He puts the ring in the palm of her hand.
And she puts her hand over his.
They hold all four hands.
And look at each other.)

. . .

Good luck.

. . .

G

Good luck.

. . .
. . .

B & G

I'll see you soon.

(A light goes off.
Dark.)

* * *
* * *

In dark, they part.
Two people stand apart, alone, in different cities.

Weeks.
Months.

Years.

* * *
* * *

A light goes on.
Winter 2006. A few days away from a new year. Very late night.

B

(Off) Hold on Can't find my // keys—

G

(Off) Oh I've got mine.

(A key in a door.
A string of Christmas lights has been turned on.

This is what we may or may not see:
A small apartment in the Ironbound section of Newark.
A top floor of a four-story building located on a residential street, just
around the corner from the main drag.
This place belongs to people who work often and work late.
It is a mixture of things bought at the ABC Store on Ferry Street, the
Goodwill or the Kmart over the bridge in Kearny, and inherited from
roommates now long gone. And family who came over for a summer to
work, now also long gone.
On the walls are a few things brought over in a suitcase from across
an ocean many years ago, now collecting dust. Things made of straw or
wicker. Art purchased at the dollar store.
There is nothing intentionally kitschy about this place.
It is someone's genuine attempt to make a home out of the things they
have on hand or can afford.
Beyond the windows, we hear the last of the night's drinkers, a car or two
pumping merengue.
A cat walking up a fire escape.
Nighttime in a small city.

B and G enter.
Winter coats. G carries a wine bottle.
Tension between them.
B is not happy to see her. G feels it.)

(Referring to the lights) That's nice. Where's the tree?

B

Not this year. You need water?

G

(Referring to drinking more) Actually I thought we could—

B

I'm getting you water.

(He goes into the kitchen.
She, alone in the space, taking it in.)

G

Did you take it down already? The . . . ?

(He enters with water.)

Did you take it down?
. . . The Christmas tree?

B

No.
Just didn't really bother after that first year.
Or the second year.
Or the third.
(Referring to his mother / family) It's different without—

G

Right.

B

Yeah—family— So I didn't think, a tree, // y'know—

G

Right.

B

—that there was really any point.

. . .

Not you though.

G

What?

B

Different.

G

(Pleased) Yeah?

B

Still drink like // it's yer last meal.

G

Oh.

B

Like everything's just—yours.
Yeah.
Yer exactly the same.

G

Well if it's free, I'm gonna drink it. I'm not wasteful.

B

Who said that shit was free?

G

What?

B

That shit tonight was not free.

G

Wait.

B

(Continuing) None of that shit that you consumed tonight // was free.

G

Did you hafta pay for all those?

B

I woulda, yeah, if someone saw. So next time you decide to ambush me at work—

G

Next time you won't be workin when we made plans.

B

(Jab) I will always have to work.

. . .

G

Why'd you keep refillin my glass // if—

B

Had to give you something to do.

G

I came to see you.

B

Yeah but I got called into— I said we'd reschedule.

G

(*Sore point*) We did. Couple times. Been tryin to see you since I got in but said they got you workin every day.

Even Monday.
When they're closed.

B

Holiday season's different. You looked up the schedule?

G

I remember the schedule.

B

You thought I was lying // to you?

G

No.

B

Look I'm sorry—

G

It's okay.

B

(*Jab*) —I'm sorry *I* had to work.
(*"Fuck you"*) Here's yer water.

G

(*"Fuck you too"*) Thank you.

. . .

. . .

B

(Ending the night) So listen I'm gonna // need to head to bed soon—

G

Oh shit did I give you this? Here. It's wine. Merry Christmas. Belated.

B

You shouldn't have—

G

Yer welcome.

B

(Continuing) —I work at a bar.

G

Can I crash?

. . .

B

Bus is still runnin.

G

It's not actually. Not the 40. Last one left a half hour ago.

B

You need money for a cab then?

G

No.

                              B

("Bye") Okay. So.

                              G

She's got this other guy in the apartment now.

                              B

So where've you been staying?

                              G

There. While I was waiting for you.

                              B

For me to what.

                              G

Appear. Respond. I came down to see you. Not to sleep on their couch and get twenties jacked from my purse. You think I'm on vacation? Here?

                              B

Okay so if you need money—

                              G

No!

                              B

Then what.

                              G

I'm goin back in a few days.

                              B

And I've been workin all night.

                              G

I brought a bottle.

B

And thank you but do I hafta drink it now?

G

I didn't get a chance to talk to you at all // at the bar.

B

I was workin. On gettin you free // drinks.

G

I didn't want free drinks.

B

You seemed to.

G

I wanted to see you.

B

And you saw me. You saw the place. Like you wanted. You got everything you wanted—

G

How's yer mom—

B

You already asked me that. So I can walk you over to Penn and you can catch a cab—

(CRACK.
B turns back to see she's opened the wine.)

G

It's a twist off.

(An irrevocably open bottle of wine between them.)

I didn't want any barriers and/or obstacles I'll grab glasses.

*(She exits to the kitchen. Takes off her coat.
He stands there, alone. Angry to be trapped.*

G enters, with glasses, muscling an energy of Everything's Fine.)

(Reentering) It's good to be back. This place. The fire escape.
I missed this place—

B

I think you need to go home.

. . .

G

You called me down here.

B

I called you last month. And you didn't come.

G

You told me not to!

B

("Just go") It doesn't matter.

G

(Continuing) When I called you back, you told me don't come.

B

Well you had exams. So.

G

I told you I would though! I said fuck exams, soon as there's a bus,
there's no bus outta Boston at two in the morning, what could
I do—

B

It doesn't matter—

G

(Continuing) And then you said don't come—

B

And you listened. So.

G

I'm here. I'm here now.

B

Well it was nice of you to stop by on your way to a future.

G

. . .

B

Nice of you to make the time. The trip. The effort. Eventually. Nice to finally fuckin see you. You know they cost a dollar, some of these buses? From Boston. If you book early. Here.

(A dollar. Which she won't take. So he drops it before her. Cold.)

Hope your next visit will be just as pleasant.

G

Wanna practice?

. . .

B

What.

G

When did you meet?
What school?
What did the two of you have in common?—

B

Why'd you back out.
Wanna start there?
How bout Why'd you back out, wanna start there?

G

. . .

B

What.
Please.
Cuz all I got was a letter. After three years of waiting. Three and a
half years of planning. Tellin me you changed yer mind.

G

What if I changed it back?

B

Just like that.

G

I'm here.

B

So am I. I've been here. For three and a half years, I've been here.
I felt like I had the key, a key, in my hands. I never felt that before
in my entire life. I made plans. Schools. What schools I might—
Doors opened up for me, everywhere, in my mind, the things
I could imagine for myself. There were things I was finally able to
really imagine for myself. I was gonna join the world I live in. The
world you got to live in for three and a half years. And then—a
letter.

G

Stories were comin out every day, what could happen, if we were caught. Lady jailed five years, couple in Texas fined a quarter-mil—

B

I was always up-front about what you'd be risking.

G

Yeah well it didn't sink in. It didn't sink in til it did.

B

Three and a half // years—

G

Last month. At two in the morning.
It didn't sink in how much I was risking
til you called me last month,
at two in the morning,
and were finally,
actually
Up-Front.

I ignored the stories, the news, my feelings—any feelings I coulda had—for anyone else. I never even kissed anyone. For three and a half years. I wore the ring. And then you called. And it sunk in.

Cuz no.
You were not always up-front.
About everything.
No.
. . .
You shoulda told me.

B

I didn't tell anyone.

G

Yeah but you should have told *me*.

B

You knew. You always knew.

G

Yeah but—

B

That that could happen, you knew.

G

It wasn't supposed to.

B

You never asked me not to.

G

I didn't think I needed to! If it's a quarter-mil or jail!

B

Well what did you expect?—

G

For you to be smarter.

B

No one knew.

G

And not that.

B

/ / What did you expect.

G

Not a call like that—

B

What did you expect.

G

Nothing!
Congratulations.

(She takes their ring from her pocket.
Leaves it—)

I wish you both the best.

(—and moves to exit.)

B

You can crash on the couch.

(She stops.)

If you have to.
Had to get a roommate so the other room's got—

G

Shit sorry. I've been loud.

B

No she's gone this week. Got family in Philly so she's there now.
Through New Year's.
I just don't wanna go in her room while she's away.

G

No problem.

                            B
Trust, y'know. Cuz of trust.

                            G
Yeah. Couch is fine.
Or I could—

                            B
What.

                            G
No yeah couch is fine.

                            B
I'll get you sheets.

(He does. She feels strange here for the first time.
He returns with sheets. She tries to change the temperature, lower the
tension.)

                            G
Surprised you had as many people at the bar tonight. Figured
people'd be with family.

                            B
Well that's not a thing everybody has.

                            G
. . . I know that.

                            B
Oceans away, for a lotta people.
It's actually been a pretty good week for me at work. Busy, this
neighborhood.
(Referring to immigration status) There's a lot of us that can't go
home.

(He tosses sheets at her.)

You for real?

G

. . .

B

You'd do this?

(She drops the sheets.
Takes back the ring.
Looks him in the eye.
And puts it on her finger.)

When.

G

Name the day.

B

June 4th.

G

("Yer a dick") My graduation?
Okay.
June 4th.

B

Bring yer mom.

(B tests her.)

We would need one of our moms there. For photos. As a witness.

MARTYNA MAJOK

                              G
And you already have yours?
Your person.
To witness.

                              B
I thought about it. Yeah. I dunno, it might be . . .

                              G
Yeah.

            B   G
Nice.   Pretty fucked up.

. . .

                              G
So you feel safe? With your witness——?

                              B
Yeah.

                              G
——bein involved in all this? Cuz it's a lot. It'd be a lotta fuckin
trouble.

                              B
I know that.

                              G
(Continuing) This would be both our lives if we're caught.
So I would just need to know before June 4th if you feel safe.
With your witness.

                              B
I do.

G

Really.

B

Yeah.

. . .

G

Really.

B

Yeah.

. . .

(G tests him.)

G

You think we'd need to answer personal stuff in the interview?

B

Like about money?

G

Like about our bodies.

B

. . .

G

You think they'll ask about our bodies when they bring us into separate rooms?

B

Like, what our bodies are like?

G

Personal things, yeah. Things only we're supposed to know about each other.

B

Why.

G

You think they might?

B

They might, maybe.

G

So what should I know.

B

What.

G

About yer body.

B

. . .

G

I head back in a few days—

B

We don't hafta talk about this now.

G

Then when.

B

Are we really doing this?

G

When would we talk about that.

B

I don't know.
The honeymoon.
I guess we'd go over that on the honeymoon.

G

Always looked forward to that.

B

Me too.

G

Never went on vacation.

B

I'd always looked forward to it too.

. . .
. . .
. . .

G

You think we'd have to . . .

B

What?

G

. . . on the honeymoon?

. . .

B
I don't think so. Not like, actually.

G
Then you'll have to describe it to me.
What it might be like.
With you.

. . .

. . .

. . .

What do you look like.

. . .

. . .

. . .

B
. . . I um— Really?

I . . .

I have a mole here. *(Points somewhere on his chest)*
I think you saw that when we went down the shore.
And here. *(Points somewhere else on his chest)*
And . . . here. *(Gestures around an intimate area)*

G
Where?

B
There.
Here.

G

I think I have one there too.

And here. *(Points to her collarbone)*

And here. A few here. *(Points to the back of her neck)*

And here. *(Points to one of her ribs)*

And two here. *(Points to the inside of one of her thighs)*

B

You got a lot.

G

There might be more. I can check later on myself. For you.

B

Yeah I'll check on me too.

G

You have one here.

(She touches a part of his face.)

You missed that one.

What are you like? When you—

B

We're doin this right now?

G

It's the only part we haven't covered. So if you wanted to tell me—or show me—now's the time. I'm here.

I make noise when I'm—

B

Okay.

G

When I'm about to—

B

I don't think they'd ask us this—

G

What about scars.
Things that might turn into scars.
Bruises.

B

. . .

G

Any scars.
Bruises—

(Keys in a lock.
They both turn toward the sound.
A man at the door.
Henry.
Wearing an overnight backpack, carrying a paper bag.
He sees a woman in the apartment—and freezes.)

. . .
. . .

HENRY

Sorry wrong apartment.

(Henry exits.)

B

You don't have to—
("Come back") Henry!

. . .

(Henry stops. Returns.)

HENRY

Did I just fuck everything // up?

B

No no no it's okay, come in.

HENRY

I tried calling—

B

I've been at work since four. // Didn't get a chance—

HENRY

Since four? You can't keep doing this to yourself.

B

I know. "Wrong apartment"?

HENRY

Well it was either that or, *(Referring to the paper bag)* "Somebody order delivery?"
From apparently that restaurant that's got everybody's house keys.
Chicken parm.
Surprise.

B

Aw.

(The two men kiss. Committed lovers.)

HENRY

I was getting nervous something happened.

B

Something did.

(B gestures toward G.
And now Henry recognizes her.)

HENRY

. . .

G

. . .

HENRY

Is this . . . ?

G

Yeah.

. . .
. . .

HENRY

("Look at that") Huh.

G

What.

HENRY

Uh-huh.

G

What.

HENRY

. . .

G

. . .

B

. . .

HENRY

(To G) Can you excuse us?—

G

No thank you.

B

(To G) Could you though?
Fer like, a minute?

G

. . .

. . .

. . .

. . .

. . .

. . .

(Eventually, she moves to exit—stops, turns back to take her wine glass with her, showily mistrustful of Henry—and continues to exit.

B and Henry watch her disappear into the bathroom until they think she can't hear them.
Then turn to one another.)

HENRY

I thought we weren't doing this anymore.

B

She just showed up at the bar, then she asked to come up, I didn't think she was gonna wanna crash—

HENRY

She's spending the night?

B

I wasn't planning on it but—

HENRY

What's she doing here.

B

Visiting.

HENRY

But what's She said she didn't wanna do this.

B

She changed her mind.

. . .

HENRY

(*"We're not doing this"*) No.

B

It's a lot to ask someone to risk a quarter-mil and five years in jail.

HENRY

It's a lot to ask of you. To hold out hope for // all this time—

B

What's our other option? What other option do I have? Marry you?

HENRY

I wish you could.

B

Well I wish a lotta shit.

I can't wait for something that might never happen.

I can't watch all my days disappear into a stupid under-the-table restaurant job on Ferry Street. I panic every time I jaywalk I'll get locked up in a fuckin detention center.

HENRY

So don't jaywalk.

B

I want to start my life. My life ... I'm losing it.

She's goin back in a few days. Tonight might be my only chance—

HENRY

Why don't we just ask one of my // friends—

B

No one knows me like she does. No one else could do this.

HENRY

We need to talk about— Just— // hold on.

B

She'd be doin a huge thing for me. For us.

HENRY

And when she backs out? I can't watch you go through that // again—

B

I'll be fine.

HENRY

You were not fine, baby, I was there. You barely left the bed for a week. This whole month, you've // been a ghost.

B

I'll be fine.

HENRY

(Continuing) Every time you don't pick up your phone, I think I'll
find you // in the bathtub—or the closet—

B

It's not a big deal if she crashes.

HENRY

To who it's not a big deal?

G

(Returning) I brought wine.

HENRY

Oh are we staying up?

B

(To Henry) If that's okay?

G

But you can go, Henry.
If yer tired.

HENRY

No I'm awake.

G

We were gonna practice a little. I dunno if he told you—

HENRY

He told me, yeah, that you're reconsidering.

G

So you can go home.

. . .

HENRY

Y'know what:

(WINE. Henry brought a bottle too. A nice one.)

Let's all have a glass. Get to know each other. You and I don't really, y'know, know everything there is to know about each other. We can talk about the honeymoon—

G

Oh we talked about—

HENRY

Since I'd be coming on the honeymoon.

(G looks at B.)

. . .

B

. . . I was gonna mention . . .

HENRY

(A bad joke) I mean I gotta get something out of all this!

G

You'd be getting a lot.

HENRY

So would you. Did you decide on a number?

245

                          B
Let's // start over.

                          G
A what?

                     HENRY
Your fee.

                          G
For what.

                     HENRY
Your services.

. . .

                          G
I don't want money.

                     HENRY
I think you will once you're outta that school 'n' back in this
world.
It's not easy out here.

          G   B
I know.   She knows, Henry.

                     HENRY
You'll be paying off that school a while.

                          G
I'm on scholarship.

                     HENRY
So was I. And then I graduated. You know it's not all scholarship,
right?

                              G

What.

                            HENRY

When they say you got an award, it's not necessarily a scholarship.
Sometimes those awards are loans.

                              G

(Had no idea) . . . yeah I know.

                            HENRY

You might wanna look into that.
We insist. On paying you.
If you actually did this . . . we'd insist. Cuz it would be a lotta work.
Lotta time. Some money would be helpful along the way. Like if
you need a hotel.

                              B

("Can you not?") okay

                            HENRY

So no one ever loved you?

              G   B

Wow.   Okay. // Starting over.

                            HENRY

(Continuing) You don't believe in love?

                              G

I do.

                            HENRY

You never wanted to get married?

                              G

I am getting married.

247

HENRY

I mean really.

G

We would be. Really.

HENRY   B

Not really, no.   I mean, not really really.

G

I think we'd hafta do it pretty really.

HENRY

Cuz of your mom?

G

. . .

HENRY

Is that why you never wanted to get married—really? Never seen
it go well?

G

(To B) What else you tell him?

HENRY

Did they love each other?

G

Who.

HENRY

Your examples. Of folks for whom it didn't go well. In marriage.

G

For whom, // wow.

HENRY

You go to school in Boston, fuck yeah for fuckin whom.

G

I think they did, yeah.
I think they really did, yeah, once.

HENRY

And what happened?

G

(Finality) A lot.
. . .
Maybe some people shouldn't marry for love.
For what they say is love. At first.
Some people maybe it's better they marry for other things.

HENRY

(As if Boston were G's name) Like what, Boston.

G

Kindness.
Respect.
Some "love" can maybe blind yer respect.

HENRY

It shouldn't.

G

No.
It shouldn't.
Should it.

HENRY

Yeah maybe you shouldn't marry really. If that's how you think of love. Maybe a situation like this would be the best option for you actually.

G

A situation like what.

HENRY

(Referring to B's desire) Something that would never . . . y'know.

Me, I always wished I could.
Marry.
For love.

(B draws to Henry. Affection.
G watches, feeling outside of it.)

G

Yeah well it's too bad you can't.

So listen you got me here the rest of the night, *(Referring to B)* yer workin all the time and I'm in class or studyin or work-studyin all the time—

HENRY

so busy

G

(Continuing) So if you really wanna do this—

HENRY

Why the sudden change of mind.

G

What.

HENRY

Why are you here.

. . .

G

(To B) To help someone.

. . .

B

(To both) You wanna practice?

HENRY

(To B) Can I talk to you in private?

G

Nope.

HENRY

My face was not speaking to your face.

G

Nothing can be private between us.

HENRY

Among us, Boston.

G

If we're really doing this, then nothing can be private. There's people whose only job it is to smell out deception in exactly what we'd be doing. So nothing can be private—anymore—among us.

HENRY

(To B) I don't like this.

G

Then what would you like, Henry?
How would you like to help the man you wish you could marry for love?

HENRY

By marrying him.

G

Well that's a solid plan.

HENRY

It passed in Massachusetts.

G

States don't // count. Not for citizenship.

HENRY

I know that.

G

(Continuing) Not even for a green card.

HENRY

I know that. Obviously I know. Still, just the fact of Massachusetts—

G

One state.

HENRY

Is a huge deal.

G

One state and nothing since. You need the whole country to
agree—all fifty // states—first to even let you marry and then
for that to count—

HENRY

—to recognize, Correct, on the national level and then for that to
count for citizenship, I know.

                    G
Yeah? What do you know about it?

                    B
Henry goes to law school.

. . .

                    G
No he doesn't.

                 HENRY
Yeah I really do though.

. . .

                    G
Where.

(Henry's pleased she asked.
He presents his ID.
She walks up to it.
Sees the school is impressive and she hates that.)

. . .
. . .

I heard the buildings are ugly.

                    B
Henry actually knows a lot about this. He coached his parents for
the citizenship test—in high school—

                    G
Oh yeah that's nice so what's his solution for you? Just wait it out
for Alabama, Arkansas, and the other forty-seven to agree? For
that DREAM Act, any news?

I can offer you something actual. Something concrete and now, not just some hope for Someday Maybe.

HENRY

And all for free.

G

I never wanted money.

HENRY

And you'd close up shop? For the entire two-year waiting period—after a wedding—and the entire three-year period—after the interview—you'd close up shop? For five-plus years?

G

Been doin it these past three.

HENRY

Have you?

G

And a half, yeah.
(To B) No one's gotten any calls about *me* at two in the morning.

HENRY

So what's in it for you?

G

I made a promise.

HENRY

Three and a half years ago.

G

That's right.

HENRY

But you're here now.

Why didn't you do it earlier? I'm just curious. Before you left.
Or after your first semester. Your first year. Second. Third. Why
didn't you do it as soon as you could?—

G

Cuz we're doin it now.

HENRY

Uh-huh.
I'm not going anywhere.

G

Okay.

HENRY

I'm part of this.

G

We'll see but okay.

B

He is.
I'd like him to be.

HENRY

(To B) I am.

G

Fine. Then I guess you'll both have to agree. You have to agree—
both of you—that I'm the only person who could do this. Well
enough to not get caught. Decent enough not to just take your
money and run. Or extort you. Good enough to let you be a part
of this, Henry. To do any of this at all.

HENRY

If you // do it.

G

(Continuing) You'd both need to agree if three and a half years has
been a long enough test of all that.

HENRY

Til you found out about me, // it seems, and called it off.

G

Right.

Til I found out. About you. After you'd been together—apparently—for years. Two—that I know of. Makin decisions about
me, for me, while I knew nothing. And had no one. And all while
you've been at law school, Henry—harboring a criminal. Techni-
cally. Aiding and abetting THIS. *(Referring to herself and B)* A felony.

I mean, from the outside, it might even look like I was purpose-
fully misled. Doesn't it? From the outside, I mean. To a court of
law.

HENRY

. . .

G

I guess you'd both need to agree I'm the best option he has. To
start his life.

That is, if that's something you would like. If that's something you
would like, Henry, for the man you say you wish you could marry
for love.

. . .

. . .

HENRY

Okay y'know what. There's some fuckin cheese in the fridge. I'm
gonna put it on a fuckin plate 'n' we're gonna eat it—

B

. . . That brie I brought from work?

HENRY

Did you eat it.

. . .

Here then Here's some chicken fuckin parm Do you know he
loves chicken // parm—

G

I do.

HENRY

Please excuse me while I plate this shit Wine?

G

Please.

HENRY

Yer welcome.

B

("I'm sorry") Henry—

HENRY

I want what's best for you.
I want you happy.
But you need to be sure this is how.

(Henry exits to the kitchen.

B and G alone. A strange air between them.

G is pleased to have won the moment—then feels B pull away.
B is aware how much this is costing Henry. He's angry to be in this situation. And so, ices G out.)

. . .
. . .

G

(Trying to connect) When did we meet?

. . .

B

. . .
. . .

G

What school?

B

. . .
. . .

G

Where was it located?

B

Hundred Davis.

G

In?

B

. . .
. . .

G

What's the best pizza in town?
What did the two of you have in common?——

B

Not much anymore.

(Henry enters, behind them. Watches.)

G

What's your favorite aspect of your partner?
You remember our old answer?

B

Her kindness.

G

What did the // two of you——

B

(Continuing) Was our old answer.

HENRY

You met in Miss Ramirez's class. ESL. Third grade. You forgot your lunch. She shared hers. You brought extra the next day to pay her back. Your idea. You were the only two students to move up to English-speaking classes that next year. Both your favorite color's blue. Cobalt. Teal. And the best pizza in town was Joe's.

Is.
Joe's.

What else should I know?
As your witness?

B

(Quiet love) thank you

HENRY

First "date"?

G

Well we've known each other forever so. It's hard to really pin-
point // exactly—

HENRY

(To B) Is that how she's gonna respond? *(To G)* Is that how you're
gonna respond?
First date.

G

The movies. Two-for-one Tuesday.

HENRY

Which was when.

G

'98. Let's say—

HENRY

When exactly.

G

Summer. Junior high.

HENRY

What's each other's shoe size.

B	G
Both of us? Fuck—eight?	Like, current shoe—nine?
Six?	Ten!

HENRY

(To G, a brag) He's a twelve.
Brand of shampoo, both of you, go.

B	G
Um . . .	I can . . . check.

HENRY

Deodorant.

B	G
Really?	Old Spice?

HENRY

Brand of toothpaste.

B	G
Wouldn't we use the same one?	We can just make a list of this stuff.

HENRY

Yes, Love, ideally, that's what you'd both answer.
What's your favorite aspect of your partner.

G	B
His kindness.	Her— . . . yeah.

HENRY

When did you decide to get married?

G	B
High school.	Right after high school. Not long after.

HENRY

Who proposed to *whom*.

B

I did.

G

He did. My last day in town.

HENRY

Where. How.

B

At the bus stop.

G

He waited with me at the bus.

B

Her last day in town.

G

I didn't wanna go.

B

My mom left a ring.
I carried it around for days cuz I knew she was leavin for school.

G

You did?

B

In my pocket. I safety-pinned it inside my pocket so it wouldn't
fall out.
I carried it for days.

G

He proposed at the bus.

B

Her last day in town.

G

I didn't wanna go.

B

My mom left a ring.

G

(Genuine) I didn't wanna go.

B

I carried it around for days cuz I knew she was leaving.

G

He was always there when I needed him.

B

She was—

She was always there.
When I needed her.

G

(Genuine) . . . What did you do while she was away?

B

I worked.
Saved.

G

Wasn't much money to visit. But we talked all the time.

B

A lot of the time, yeah. We'd talk.

G

I sent postcards.

B

She sent postcards.

G

And books.

B

Thank you.

G

From my classes. Yer welcome.
She'd call. At night.
Every night.
Before she went to bed, she'd call.

B

I took the bus up to Boston once. To see her.

G

. . . He took the bus up to—

B

But she didn't see me.

. . .

. . .

I took a bus.
The T.
And I walked to her campus to find her.

I snuck into a class. I smelled the books. I sat on leather. I watched
the people. I felt the life. Someone let me in a door. Thought
I was a student. Just forgot my ID. They let me in. Didn't think
twice, they let me in. I listened to lectures. I raised my hand.
I answered a question. About a book I'd read. Coincidence, I'd
read that book. I got it right. The question. Very right. Made

people wonder who was, who's this guy, people wondered who
I was. I found the dining hall. Someone swiped me in. Forgot my
ID, I said, so they let me in. Didn't think twice. I ate the food.
I went for seconds. I ate dessert. I touched the stone. I walked
the grass. I passed by windows. I heard the laughs. I watched the
night. And I went home.

. . .
. . .

G

Did you see her?

B

I did.

G

But she didn't see you?

B

No.

G

What if she did.
What would you have done.

. . .
. . .

B

I would have walked away.
Let her pretend she didn't see me.
I'd never take that away.
The trees. The books.
As much as I . . .
I couldn't.

...
...

... Why'd you stay away?

G

...

B

(Not unkindly) ... All this time.
Why'd you stay away.

G

Money.
Time. And money.

(B is disappointed and further saddened by her answer.)

Guilt.
About the trees and the books.
Guilt about not loving it up there.
When that's all you ever wanted.
And guilt about loving it.
Sometimes.

...
...

I'm sorry.

...
...

B

(Heartbroken) It's ...

(He can't say "okay.")

. . .

HENRY
When did your relationship turn romantic.

. . .

(B looks back at Henry,
who has been witnessing a genuine relationship . . .
and is becoming concerned.)

. . .

B
She used to climb up my fire escape at night. And I'd sneak her into my bedroom.

HENRY
They'll want more details than that.

B
I don't think they will.

HENRY
I think they very likely might, My Love, if that's how you're gonna answer.

B
This didn't actually happen.

HENRY
Well don't tell them that.
When did your relationship turn romantic.

B

She used to climb up my fire escape at night and I'd sneak her into
my bedroom and one night . . .

HENRY

Yeah?

B

—it turned romantic.

G

I used to climb up his fire escape at night and he'd sneak me into
his bedroom and one night, as we're layin there, close cuz his bed's
a twin, one night as we're layin there, I feel his breath on my neck.

And it feels like he's peelin back my skin.
Just from his breath on my neck.
He says my name.
He knows I'm awake but he says my name.
And then we

B

Yeah.
And then we.

G

Yeah.

. . .
. . .

HENRY

You've really created a little . . . Yeah . . . world. For yourselves.

I'm nowhere in your story.

. . .

268

B

... Well ... no ...
Really?

HENRY

I'm gonna be nowhere in your ...

B

I'm not doin this for fun.

HENRY

I know.
It's just a thing I'm fully realizing.
That's all.

G

How long have you known each other.

HENRY

Two years. And a half. // Almost.

G

No, me and him.
How long have you known each other.

...

HENRY   B
Since third grade.   Thirteen years.

G

Two-thirds of our lives.
First kiss?

B

(Concerned about Henry) I don't remember when we said.

G

May 22nd.
What's your favorite aspect of your partner.

B

His kindness.

HENRY

. . .

B

(Moving to him) His ambition. His intellect. His body. His mouth.
His kindness.
First kiss: First day. June. In the city. I missed my train. Last one
of the night. On purpose.
How many lies have you had to tell for me. How much have
I asked of you—

HENRY

It's okay.

B

How late would I call and how quick would you pick up—

(Henry kisses B. "It's okay.")

G

What's yer favorite part of her body.

B

No we're done.

G

What's yer favorite part of // her body.

B

We're done.

G

His mouth. What's yer favorite part of // her body.

B   HENRY

Her hands.   *(To B)* You don't have to do this.

G

I'm not convinced. Did your parents approve of the match Why
or why not Why or why not Did your mother fuckin wish we
were sleepin together?

. . .

B

(Wounded) That's not why she left.

HENRY

(To B) We don't have to // do this. Not like this.

G

I'm not convinced.

B

She left cuz it was harder here for her—

HENRY   G

It would be years of this.   I'm not convinced.

B

—and cuz of September—

HENRY

Baby, do you want *years* // of this?

B

I never wanted any of this. I never wanted to have to do any of this.
For this to be my only option—

G

Tell me about his body, Henry. // In case they ask.

B

No.

G

(Continuing) Anything distinct I should know? Any scars, //
bruises—

B

No, we're done for the night.

G

(Continuing) Anything like that? Scars? Bruises? You know he
called me that night—

HENRY

Okay.

G

(Continuing) Middle of the night, cold as hell he said— He called
me from a pay phone and said someone had kicked him out //
without his shoes.

HENRY

I didn't kick him out—

G

(Continuing) He was walkin around Newark at night in the cold
without his shoes—

HENRY   B

We had a fight.   I left.

G

And you kick him out without his shoes? It's his apartment.

B

He didn't— // I just—

G

(Continuing) You called me! He // called me!

B

I called you Yeah I called but you weren't here. You stayed in Boston.

G

I told you to go to my mom's.

B

I wasn't gonna go to yer mom's in the middle of the night.

G

You coulda come to Boston.

B

I had no shoes!

G

What did you do that night?

B

I went to a diner and waited til the Kmart opened, bought some shoes, and went to work. I just—I needed to talk that night. To someone. To you. We had a fight—

HENRY

We had a fight and now we're fine people fight. But do you know what he did when you backed out? I couldn't get him to eat. Shower. He wouldn't leave the bed for a fuckin week.

G

I got nervous.

HENRY

No you became aware of what this really is. This isn't some game, some fuckin fantasy. This shit is for real.

G

Then why the fuck did I not even know about you til a fuckin month ago?—

HENRY

Prob'ly cuz he knew it'd go THIS well.

G

First time I ever heard your damn name was over sobbing on a pay phone! I got nervous cuz who the fuck was fuckin Henry—

HENRY

I am.

G

—and would he risk a quarter-mil and five years in jail?

HENRY

I *am*.

G

Not like I am. You could deny. You could say you didn't know. You could step away.

HENRY

I haven't.

G

You don't have to risk a quarter-mil // and five years in jail—

HENRY

I would if I could.

G

(Continuing) —just to help somebody.

HENRY

You'd be getting paid.

G

Would you risk all that just to help someone?

HENRY

Yes.

G

Okay so you go marry someone.

HENRY   B
I don't— What—   What?!

G

If it's so easy then you go marry // someone and help her—

HENRY

What are you even— This isn't a trade.

G

Then you can't know how scary this is. You can't tell me shit about this.

275

B

He's not marrying anybody.

HENRY

Unless it's you.

G

WHICH YOU NEVER WILL. YOU WILL NEVER DO THAT.
YOU WILL NEVER BE ABLE TO EVER LEGALLY DO THAT
IN THIS COUNTRY. IT'S 2000 FUCKIN 6 ALMOST 7 IN A
FEW FUCKIN DAYS SO IF IT HASN'T HAPPENED NOW IT
NEVER FUCKIN WILL. YOU WON'T EVER, EVER MARRY
HIM.

. . .
. . .
. . .

HENRY

Well.
Neither will you.

G

I'm helping.

HENRY

You seem to want love so fuckin bad, you'd settle for it fake.

G

. . .

HENRY

The only reason someone takes someone's fuckin shoes is so they
stay.

276

I didn't want him goin out in the middle of the night in fuckin November. You think I wanted that? I went out to look for him. All night. While *you* stayed in Boston. I knew. I suspected. But he said no. She's not like that. I knew but he kept saying She's not like that. And so we had a fight. We had a fight that night—about you. And then you backed out. And you proved me right. I wish you coulda seen what that did to him, your backing out, cuz then you'd never put him through that again. You wanna help? You're here to help? Yeah? Up to what point?

G

. . .

HENRY

(To B) Do we have to do this? Is all this worth it?

B

(Lost) I've been hiding and lying for the past thirteen years of my For every For just basic human Because I didn't get some Some paper means I cannot be a full person here. I have had to hide who I am at every fuckin turn of my life—

HENRY

I know that.

B

—I've been lying so long I'm not even sure what's real.

HENRY

Then maybe you should question a couple things in your life.

G

Yeah maybe you should question a really major thing in yer life. If you don't know what's real.

B

. . .

G

I got nervous and I'm sorry but I'm here. I'm ready to risk a quarter-mil, jail, whatever future I might have—for you. So you can be a full person here.

HENRY

And what's that gonna cost him.

G

You.

. . .

(To B) I don't trust him.

B

You don't know him.

G

That's not my fault.

B

If you'da come down any time in the last year you would've met him.

G

Not even his name. That he existed. I didn't even know a Henry existed.

B

(Referring to his sexuality) But you always knew—

G

Not that a Henry was currently existing. Currently stealing your shoes and // doin who-knows-what-else to you—

B

We had a fight——once——

G

Didn't seem like just a fight when you called. I never heard those kinda sounds outta you——

B

And you didn't come.

G

I'm here now.

B

You never heard those sounds and still you didn't // come.

G

You wanted me to take a bus in the middle of the night from Boston?

B

YES.
How can I trust you?

G

(Lunges for him) Take off yer shirt.

B

What. // No.

G

Take yer clothes off. Lemme see what "once" looks like.
// Lemme take a look at Henry's "once."

B

That's not what this is.

G

(Continuing) My mother denied it too // til she got naturalized—

HENRY

I'm not like your house.

G

(Continuing) Kept thinkin he'd follow her, blackmail her, fuckin, disappear her, who'd know? Who'd care about her fuckin— unregistered body somewhere?

B

Henry was here when you weren't.

G

I was always here.

B

You weren't!

I promised myself I wouldn't take anything else. Told myself, She'd be doin this huge thing for you—for the rest of your life—so don't ask a thing more of hers. Don't ask to come up. Or for her to come down. But three and a half years . . . I thought you'd at least have wanted to.

But you had something to lose.
You found something more than just me . . . to lose.

It's a beautiful world up there. Boston. If I were you, I might not have come back either. But it's ending. It's ending soon.

Where you gonna crash when life breaks for you next.
Or has it already?

. . .

G

You better be sure Henry's worth ten-hour shifts on yer feet. Not seein yer mother for years. The crushing fuckin panic every time you see a cop. You better be sure he's worth me walkin out. I hope your secret fuckin boyfriend of two and a half years would be worth every second of Fish Kill fuckin Road.

What's it gonna be.

. . .

. . .

. . .

(B becomes nervous.)

. . .

B

Why won't you say anything.

HENRY

I can't choose for you.

B

. . .

HENRY

If all your days disappear into an under-the-table restaurant job on Ferry Street, you'll resent me.

B

No—

HENRY

As much as I'd like to, I can't be the one to choose this.

B

Why do I have to?

HENRY

I didn't make the terms.

. . .

(B looks at Henry. At G.
At Henry.
At G.)

B

You would go ahead with a wedding?, with all the tests, questions?
With livin with me, livin in Newark, with all the hiding, the lying,
the risks, for two more years—at least—and who knows how
much longer after that, you'd do that?

G

Yeah.

B

You'd do all that?
If I throw Henry out of my life?

G

Yeah.

B

Then no.

G

. . .

B

No.

. . .

(G understands this means an end.)

G

Third grade
Franklin
Hundred Davis
Kearny
He waited with me at the bus
Carried it around for days in his pocket
My last day in town
His kindness

(She removes the ring.
And returns it to B's hands,
as he had once placed it into hers.)

Good luck.

(G moves to gather her things. Moves to exit.)

HENRY

(To B) I'm sorry.

B

It's. . .

(He can't say "okay.")

HENRY

We could ask one of my friends——

B

No.
I don't want to do this again.

Maybe we can just . . . live our life somewhere else.
If it's this or Fish Kill Road.
Maybe I can finally see my mom.

Would you come with me?
If I had to move back?

(G stops at the door, turns back.
Henry clocks he's being watched by G. And B.)

Would you // come?

> HENRY

Let's get ready for bed.

. . .
. . .

To live?

> B

Yeah.

> HENRY

Really?
. . .
We never talked about this.

> B

We're talking about it now.

> HENRY

What would we do there?

> B

We'd live our lives, a version of our lives, like we've been living here.

HENRY

There is no version of my—
Let's talk in the // morning.

B

Henry.

HENRY

I'm going to school here. Studying the laws of here. What would
I do there?

B

You could go to school there, study there—

HENRY

Baby. I know like, all of two words of—

B

I didn't speak English when I first came. You'd learn.

HENRY

My family's all here.

B

You can visit your family. They can visit you.

HENRY

Wouldn't it just be more hiding?
Another version of hiding. There. For you and me.
I've done so much of that. For so much of my life.
I lost too much of my life already to that. Even before this. I'm
done with that.

B

I know but— Maybe—

285

HENRY

We never talked about this.

B

Why would you want to stay in a country that doesn't want me in it?

(Henry realizes something. And it breaks his heart.)

HENRY

This isn't gonna stop.
No matter what you choose, this isn't gonna stop.
You never talked about going back before. You never wanted to.
And if you did, you'd blame me—

B

No.

HENRY

You would. And if you don't go through with this—with her—
then every night you came home and nothing's changed, it'd be
my fault.

B

No. Just—

HENRY

(Continuing) It'd be my fault you stayed.

B

Let's just go to bed.

HENRY

(Continuing) And if you left, that would be my fault.

B

Just forget I even—

HENRY

We wouldn't make it.
Here or there.
And if you leave, you won't be allowed back.
And all of that would be my fault.
I'm sorry.

B

No— Listen— Just— We'll keep living how we've been living—

HENRY

She should stay.

B

Henry—please.

(B clings to Henry, trying to hold him here in some way.)

HENRY

This was never for me. So you could stay with me.
You were never doin this for you and me.

(Henry softly pulls away from B.

B feels abandoned—again.
And he throws Henry away.
Henry looks at B. At his back.)

(A gift) It was never for me.

(Henry turns to exit. Sees G there.)

(A curse) But it was definitely never for you.

(And Henry exits.

287

B stands there, an island of grief.
And then he sees G.)

. . .
. . .
. . .

B
. . . You gonna need another blanket?
Or is that enough,
what I set out?

. . .

G
I can just catch a cab.

B
Yer not gonna stay?

G
I don't think I should be doin this.

. . .

B
"This"?

G
. . . stayin over.

B
Is that what you meant when you said "this" the first time? Stayin
over? You shouldn't be stayin over?

G
. . .

B

Please.

G

Maybe you should think about things a little // more—

B

No. Please.

G

Why don't we talk in April // when—

B

No.

G

During break. If I'm back. Maybe we could . . . talk again then.
. . . What are you doin for New Year's?

B

Workin. Just stay the night—

G

It'll be light out soon. I could also just walk.

B

You could stay here.

G

I know.
I know.
(Referring to ending up here) I could.

I'll call you in April?

B

Only if you—

. . .

G

(An end) Okay.

I really liked practicing.

B

I know.

G

I really liked . . . our time.

B

Please don't call.

G

Okay.
. . . Happy—

. . .

B

You can say it.

G

Happy New Year.

B

Thank you.

G

(Genuine) Happy New Year.
And
Good luck.

(G exits.

B is alone.

The sounds of an empty apartment and a small city, beyond the windows.

B holds the ring.

B goes to the window.

The sounds of the small city outside fill the apartment.
The light of approaching day.)

B

when did you
decide
what do you have in
when did your
relationship
did your parents
why or
have you ever had
have you ever
. . .
what are you gonna

(The sounds and lights of another day,
another night,
another week,
another year,
years.
Years passing by a young man in a small city.

But still,
he continues.)

what are you gonna

(Lights.)

END OF PLAY

Polish Translations for *Ironbound*

Page 33

POLISH: *No kurdy . . .*
TRANSLATION: Well damn . . .
PRONUNCIATION: no, koor-DEH

Page 34

POLISH: *Dobra, to dziś zrobię Ci coś / / co—*
TRANSLATION: Arright, so tonight I'll do something to you that— [Unspoken: drives you crazy / you've never seen before]
PRONUNCIATION: dobrah, to jeesh zrob-yeh chee tsosh tso

POLISH: *Roztopię Cię, kobieto—*
TRANSLATION: I'll melt you, woman—
PRONUNCIATION: roz-TOP-yeh cheh, kob-YEH-to

Page 38

POLISH: *No, Darju, ty nie rozumiesz—*
TRANSLATION: No, Darja, you don't get it—
PRONUNCIATION: no, DAR-yu, ty nyeh roz-OO-myesh

Pages 44

POLISH: *Czerwony jak cegła, rozgrzany jak piec, Muszę mieć, / / muszę ją mieć—*

TRANSLATION: Red as a brick, hot as an oven, I've gotta have, I've gotta have her—

PRONUNCIATION: chair-VONY yak tseg-WAH, roz-GSHANY yak pyets, Moosh-eh myech, moosh-eh yo myech

Page 48

POLISH: Okay, *może teraz nie jest / / najlepszy czas—*

TRANSLATION: Maybe now is not the / / best time—

PRONUNCIATION: mo-ZEH ter-AHZ nyeh yest nahy-LEHP-sheh chahs

Note: the ż in "może" sounds like the s in "pleasure."

Page 84

POLISH: *Joj.*

TRANSLATION: Ow.

PRONUNCIATION: Yohy.

Page 118

POLISH: *Nie idź! Proszę cię. Ja nie mogę. Nie mogę sama. Sama nie mogę. Kochanie . . .*

TRANSLATION: Don't go! Please. I can't. I can't alone. Alone, I can't. My Love . . .

PRONUNCIATION: Nyeh eej! Prosh-eh chee. Yah nyeh mogeh. Nyeh mogeh. Sama nyeh mogeh. Ko-HAN-yeh.

MARTYNA MAJOK was born in Bytom, Poland, and raised in Jersey and Chicago. She was awarded the 2018 Pulitzer Prize for Drama for her play *Cost of Living*, which was nominated for the Tony Award for Best Play in 2023. Other plays include *Sanctuary City*, *Queens*, and *Ironbound*, which have been produced throughout the world. Other awards include the Obie Award for Playwriting, the Arthur Miller Foundation Legacy Award, the Hull-Warriner Award, the American Academy of Arts and Letters' Benjamin Hadley Danks Award for Exceptional Playwriting, the Off Broadway Alliance Award for Best New Play, the Lucille Lortel Award for Outstanding Play, the Hermitage Greenfield Prize (first female recipient in drama), the Champion of Change Award from New York City's Mayoral Office, the Francesca Primus Prize, two Jane Chambers Playwriting Awards, the Lanford Wilson Award, the Lilly Awards' Stacey Mindich Award, the Helen Merrill Award for Playwriting, the Charles MacArthur Award for Outstanding Original New Play from the Helen Hayes Awards, the Jean Kennedy Smith Playwriting Award, the Ashland New Plays Festival Women's Invitational Prize, the David Calicchio Emerging American Playwright Prize, the Steinberg Distinguished Playwright Award, the Global Age Project Prize, a New York Theatre Workshop 2050 Fellowship, the National New Play Network (NNPN) Smith Prize for Political Playwriting, and the Merage Foundation Fellowship for the American Dream. Martyna studied at Yale School of Drama, Juilliard, University of Chicago, and New Jersey public schools. She was a 2012–2013 NNPN playwright-in-residence, the 2015–2016 PoNY Fellow at the Lark Play Development Center, and a 2018–2019 Hodder Fellow at Princeton University. Martyna wrote the libretto for a musical adaptation of *The Great Gatsby*, with music by Florence Welch and Thomas Bartlett, has developed TV projects for HBO, and is writing feature films for Plan B/Pastel/MGM and Participant.